CY

HISTORIC SPEECHES OF AFRICAN AMERICANS

HISTORIC SPEECHES OF AFRICAN AMERICANS

Introduced and Selected by
Warren J. Halliburton

THE AFRICAN-AMERICAN EXPERIENCE
FRANKLIN WATTS
New York   Chicago   London   Toronto   Sydney

Photographs copyright ©: Martha Cooper/City Lore: p. 1; New York Public
Library: pp. 2 top, 4 top, 5, 6 top, 6 middle; Library of Congress: pp. 2 bottom,
7 bottom left, 8 bottom; University of Massachusetts Archives, University
Library, University of Massachusetts/Amherst: pp. 3, 9 bottom left; The Bett-
mann Archive: pp. 4 middle, 7 top right, 9 top right, 11 top; Courtesy of the
New York Historical Society, New York City: p. 4 bottom; Historical Pictures/
Stock Montage: p. 6 bottom; New York Public Library Schomburg Center: p. 7
bottom left; Sophia Smith Collection, Smith College: p. 7 bottom right; UPI/
Bettmann Newsphotos: pp. 8 top, 9 bottom right, 10, 11 bottom, 12 top left, 12
middle left, 12 bottom right, 12 bottom left, 13, 15, 16; Department of Special
Collections, University of Chicago Library: p. 9 top left; AP/Wide World: p. 12
top right; National Aeronautics and Space Administration: p. 14 top; James
Daggs, Impact Visuals: p. 14 bottom.

Library of Congress Cataloging-in-Publication Data

Historic speeches of African Americans / introduced and selected
    by Warren J. Halliburton.
        p.   cm. — (The African-American experience)
    Includes bibliographical references and index.
    Summary: Presents speeches by various African American
    religious and political leaders from the days of slavery to the
    present, along with biographical information and historical
    background.
        ISBN 0-531-11034-6
        1. Afro-Americans—History—Sources—Juvenile
    literature. 2. Speeches, addresses, etc., American—Afro-
    American authors—Juvenile literature. [1. Afro-Ameri-
    cans—History—Sources.] I. Halliburton, Warren J.
    II. Series.
    E184.6.H57   1993
    815'.0108896073—dc20   92-39318 CIP AC

ACKNOWLEDGMENTS

Marcus Garvey: "The Principles of the Negro Improvement Association." Reprinted with permission of Atheneum, an imprint of Macmillan Publishing Company, from *Philosophy and Opinions of Marcus Garvey, or Africa for the Africans*, edited by Amy Jacques-Garvey. Copyright © 1923, 1925 by Amy Jacques-Garvey.

James Baldwin: "A Talk to Teachers." Copyright © 1985 by James Baldwin. From the book *The Price of the Ticket*, and reprinted with permission from St. Martin's Press, Inc., New York, NY.

Martin Luther King: "I Have a Dream." Reprinted by permission of Joan Daves Agency. Copyright © 1963 by Martin Luther King, Jr.

Malcolm X: "Address to Mississippi Youth." Reprinted by permission of Pathfinder Press. Copyright © 1965 by Betty Shabazz and Pathfinder Press.

CONTENTS

INTRODUCTION:

DECLARATIONS FOR INDEPENDENCE

Harvard University–educated historian W. E. B. Du Bois, who was also a founder of the National Association for the Advancement of Colored People (NAACP), once wrote that African-American history shows how much African Americans are divided over racial origins, on the one hand proud of African ancestry and on the other hand equally proud of American nationality. Writes Du Bois:

> The history of the American Negro is the history of this strife—this longing to attain self-conscious manhood, to merge his double self into a better and truer self. He simply wishes to make it possible for a man to be both a Negro and an American, without being cursed and spit upon by his fellows, without having the doors of Opportunity closed roughly in his face.[1]

When African Americans have spoken publicly of this longing, what they have said has survived and become a formal record of American history.

AN AFRICAN TRADITION

For African Americans, the largest racial minority in America, history and culture began in Africa and survived through oral traditions. What saved the spirit of African Americans through slavery, racism, and poverty was often a sense of themselves sharing an identity as an African people. Slaves found strength in numbers—a strength if only in the sense that each one knew they suffered as a group, not alone.

Slaves acquired the sense of themselves as a group in African traditions of storytelling. When tribal languages and family ties were suppressed by white slave owners, the African folktales, in translated form, continued to be retold. In Africa, the stories had been used to relate tribal histories, as the biblical stories of the ancient Hebrew tribes were used. Daily events were memorized by official historians and record keepers called *griots*. The officials had no written language, but memorized everything, like a living computer diskette with a program full of tribal history, laws, and culture. Each tribe had its *griot*. On special occasions the *griot* recited stories (histories) of clans, families, and tribal heroes—the proud past of the tribe from its very beginning.

African-American slaves continued the tradition of the *griots*, despite harsh circumstances which discouraged all memory of African traditions, and which certainly forced the slaves to adapt the tribal traditions and change them beyond immediate recognition. What little remained of the African tribal meaning in the stories was a means of opposing slavery and affirming African-American freedom, since slaves who knew they were once African also knew that Africans in Africa were not necessarily slaves.

Today in African-American communities, one finds variations of African tribal folktales such as "The Fox and the Wolf," "The Hare, The Hyena, and The Lioness's

Cave," and "The Leopard, the Squirrel, and the Tortoise," translated into African-American dialect and orally transmitted from one generation to the next. Many contemporary African-American folktales reveal an African tribal origin (usually West African), as well as elements of African story plot, character, and theme. A common African tribal tale, which is told as a comic African-American tale, pits two animals in a battle of wits, with a smaller, weaker, more cunning character triumphing over a larger, fiercer, and dumber one.

Although entertaining and intellectually stimulating, African-American folktales were often told as lessons, or parables, of the struggle against racial oppression. The moral of the tale, at first only shared in private conversation among field slaves, soon found its way into African-American church sermons. One of the most famous sermons was "De Sun Do Move," which expressed a deep desire for freedom, promising freedom to those who had faith in a better life to come. The wisdom of the folktales became practical guides of life and a stock feature of the speeches of African Americans. As standard content of the speeches, the traditional folktales and values of African tribes survived in a hostile environment.

A distinctive language, another feature of African-American tales, developed as a result of racial segregation. Isolated from the mainstream white culture, African Americans developed a coded slang that served to disguise thoughts and feelings from whites, while the slang established a common bond of racial solidarity among African Americans.

THE AFRICAN-AMERICAN PREACHER

African-American religion was an organized social force that encouraged slave resistance and taught love of African-American people. Black preachers added to the great tradition of Southern oratory long recognized in white men of power, but what the black preachers said was not nearly as important as the spirit of their words. According to Du Bois, black slave religion featured three distinct characteristics: the Preacher, the Music, and the Frenzy. "The Preacher is the most unique personality developed on American soil. A leader, a politician, an orator, a 'boss,' an intriguer, an idealist. . . ."[2] As the first of the black orators, the preacher used the pulpit to protest as much as to preach the gospel.

Protest was not without risks. During the eighteenth century, when free black preachers were all but worshipped by their followers, slaveholders tried to use black preachers to make slaves more content, obedient, and hardworking—to teach them acceptance of their lot as slaves and contentment with their lives. Slaveholders told preachers that accepting slavery was all in the spirit of the Christian faith.

Few black preachers believed this, but they could not risk open defiance. Instead, they conducted services to suit the needs of their followers. They added spirituals and shout songs and organized secret plantation meetings. And they developed their own distinct style of preaching. While this style owed much to the African song style, in which the sentiments of the preacher were echoed by the congregation's response, the oratory of the black preacher also included some of the fancy delivery of the white politicians and preachers of Southern reputation. Altogether, a new way of worship was born, one in which the down-home preacher, either a woman or a man, shouted the Sunday morning message, appealing to a congregation that could not change real oppressive conditions but could temporarily escape them with religious fervor.

AFRICAN-AMERICAN CHURCHES AND ORGANIZATIONS

The African-American church emerged from these informal beginnings. By 1776, black Baptist churches were established in South Carolina and Virginia. A decade later, there were black Methodist churches. The growing social influence of churches was formalized in mutual aid societies that helped African Americans cope with the many hardships of city life.

These organizations provided for African Americans' needs. As David Walker wrote in the first black newspaper: "We wish to plead our own cause. Too long have others spoken for us. Too long has the publik been deceived by misrepresentations, in things, which concerns us dearly . . ."[3]

There was no more effective way for African Americans to speak for themselves than through the formal oration. Each presentation was an opportunity to spread the message of African-American freedom, first to influential white audiences and later to African Americans. African-American speeches had historical significance, and they made a lasting impression on their listeners, white and black. The African-American speakers were not simply pleading for the freedom of their people. They were using the most effective method to initiate change so that African Americans could be treated as human beings in a free society.

Before the Civil War, African Americans used the grand tradition of oratory to express their right to be free. Frederick Douglass and William Wells Brown were among the first of these orators. Often the orators differed only in the methods they advocated to overcome racism. At a convention of free blacks held in Buffalo, New York, in 1843, Henry Highland Garnet called upon slaves to stage a labor strike and to use violence in the cause of freedom. Frederick Douglass argued that such tactics would risk the lives of African Americans throughout the South.

Other speakers called for colonization of free blacks outside the United States. The colonization movement was led by sympathetic whites opposed to slavery, who saw it as a logical next step after emancipation. Some whites also saw colonization as a way to rid themselves of black troublemakers. A few African Americans supported colonization, although most opposed it. In speech after speech, they declared that the United States was their home and that African Americans had earned the right to full citizenship.

A third major difference arose concerning political action to end slavery. Members of the New England Anti-Slavery Society believed that people had only to learn the truth, and the evil of slavery would end. The more conservative New York antislavery group argued that abolishing slavery would take more than words, and called for political action. African Americans lent their support to both groups, but most recognized they had a higher calling: to work out their own solutions to the problems of achieving African-American freedom.

After 1843, the National Negro Conventions became the way. In a historic outburst of speeches, African Americans set forth militant antislavery protests never heard before. As these protests grew more focused, they resulted in petitions to Congress against violence and for new legislation for African-American equality.

Some convention members saw Abraham Lincoln as providing the solution. Others were less sure. H. Ford Douglass was foremost among this latter group. A black abolitionist from Illinois, he saw nothing in Lincoln's record to gain the support of black people against the spread of slavery. Frederick Douglass agreed, though he also realized a bitter truth: that no one better than Lincoln was available, that the Republicans were the only party to effectively oppose slavery, and that of the two political parties, the Republicans were the lesser evil.

Douglass was right. Lincoln proved himself more the politician than the great emancipator of reputation. His presidential policy was one of compromise with the pro-slavery position of white Southerners. Lincoln acted with much greater speed to preserve the Union, for example, than he did to end slavery.

What began as a war to preserve the Union, however, became a war to free the slaves. When the war began going poorly for the Northern forces, Lincoln had no alternative but to change his policy. Free slaves meant more Union soldiers. In early 1863, Lincoln issued the Emancipation Proclamation. Many African Americans insisted on their right to fight in the Civil War. African-American regiments served in the war with valor and distinction.

CONFLICT AND OUTRAGE

The end of the Civil War left two major problems: how to rebuild the Union and how to provide for the freed slaves. African Americans felt that their problems were too large to be left to white politicians. They had ideas of their own and demanded to be heard. Their voices rose as one against a new set of injustices. Carl Schurz, a white reporter investigating conditions in the South, wrote: "In portions of the northern part of [Mississippi] the colored people are kept in slavery still. The white people tell them that they were free during the war, but the war is now over, and they must go to work again as before. The reports . . . show that the blacks are in a much worse state than ever before, the able-bodied being kept at work under the lash, and the young and infirm driven off to care for themselves. As to protection from civil authorities, there is no such thing outside this city."[4]

Despite white opposition, some freedmen succeeded in acquiring land. The federally created Freedmen's Bureau assisted ex-slaves. Educating former slaves proved the Bureau's greatest success and gave a boost to African-American education.[5] With Bureau schools to educate former slaves, free elementary education among all classes in the South was established.

Freedmen's Bureau effort to provide industrial jobs to

ex-slaves was a failure. During the rebuilding of the nation known as Reconstruction, African Americans suffered a new wave of discrimination as whites who feared they would be replaced by black workers became violent. Riots broke out throughout the nation—North and South. Denied membership in national labor unions, African-American workers were powerless. They began organizing on local and state levels.

The Organization of the Colored National Labor Union, held in Union League Hall, Washington, D.C., on December 6, 1869, was the first of many conventions at which speeches described the condition of African-American workers. Race relations nevertheless worsened between blacks and whites, in industry and elsewhere. White terror and violence dramatized ill will. By 1870, the first large-scale migration of blacks from the South began. Before the end of the decade, an estimated forty thousand Southern blacks, mostly from the Gulf states of Louisiana, Mississippi, and Alabama, had moved to the Midwest.

NEW BEGINNING, OLD ENDING

Deprived of education during the long years of slavery, African Americans were eager to learn. The Freedmen's Bureau spent millions of dollars on educational programs for ex-slaves. It was not alone in this effort. Northern missionary groups founded many of the nation's most respected black colleges. African-American churches also established church colleges of their own, mostly in the South.

During the Reconstruction period, African Americans played a conspicuous role in government. They held offices in Congress and state governments throughout the South. Between 1870 and 1900, Southern states sent twenty-two African Americans to the United States Congress: two to the Senate, and twenty to the House of Representatives.

The presence of African Americans in state and federal government was not to last. By the elections of 1876, whites had regained political control of all the Southern states. Reacting to this change, the North abandoned its efforts to protect the freedmen and paved the way for a new reign of racial terror.

Seeing their civil rights violated, African Americans petitioned Congress. In 1873, at a National Civil Rights convention in Washington, D.C., George T. Downing suggested to Congress that Reconstruction laws canceling the civil rights of African Americans would discourage future racial equality and peace. Petitions that government guarantee black civil rights failed. Worse still, neither Congress nor the courts were disposed to protect the constitutional rights of black citizens.

African Americans protested the Republican party for nullifying Reconstruction policies that had established a Civil Rights Bill and the Freedmen's Bureau, and proposed amendments to the Constitution. Declaring political independence from the Republicans led in 1890 to the formation of the Afro-American League. Members of the League proposed black financial independence through the formation of their own bank. Lobbying in Washington, the League established a black presence not only to be recognized, but to be heard. And it succeeded in getting government financing for an emigration bureau to assist African Americans moving from the South into the West.

By the turn of the century, African Americans were encouraged to take one of two separate paths toward equality. One, proposed by Booker T. Washington in his famous Atlanta Exposition Address, was for African Americans to "cast down your bucket where you are."[6] What he meant was for black people to work with and develop what they already had, whether in agriculture, mechanics, commerce, or domestic service.

The other path was taken by W. E. B. Du Bois, who championed the cause of African Americans seeking all the opportunities available to whites. Many of these opportunities were in the Northern cities. Between 1910 and 1920, more than a half million African Americans left the South. They were to encounter racism in Northern cities that left many all but destitute.

Seeing neither hope nor future for black people in white America, Marcus Garvey started a "Back to Africa" movement. While the idea never succeeded, it fanned racial pride and indignation over the mistreatment of African Americans.

Black union leader A. Philip Randolph protested racism, declaring that the federal government should make all forms of racial segregation and discrimination unlawful once and for all. Randolph planned a series of Marches on Washington to pressure the government. But the entry of the United States into World War II changed black strategies. Faced with the threat to national unity by a massive African-American protest, President Franklin D. Roosevelt issued his famous executive order forbidding discrimination in war industries and government training programs. The first March on Washington was canceled.

By calling off the March on Washington, African Americans had gained the right to wartime employment: companies working under government contracts were pledged to hire African Americans or lose their contracts. But the gains made during the war were sorely tested in the postwar era. African Americans' right to vote was contested in the South as never before. And there were long legal battles to prove that public education could no longer be both separate and equal.

While some African Americans celebrated victories, others saw the injustices that remained. Many leaders spoke out against a system that passed antidiscriminatory laws but permitted racial segregation and discrimination.

CHALLENGE AND SOLUTION

While Martin Luther King, Jr., expressed his nonviolent "dream" for African Americans, Malcolm X declared the need for a black revolution. During the 1960s, the Civil Rights Movement grew into a social revolution. "Black Power" became the cry for African-American independence and equality with white society. The fight to change laws that would give African Americans equal treatment had been won. With laws changed, the problem became one of economics.

Union membership is evidence that the economic gains of African Americans have not matched successes in the Civil Rights Movement. Although black membership has increased since the 1930s, African Americans are still greatly underrepresented in trade unions. As labor leader A. Philip Randolph remarked before the civil rights revolution, "Labor's battle today is not only for bread but also for equality, status and dignity. But it does not fight for equality, status and dignity for itself alone, it fights for human dignity, the grandeur and majesty of the individual personality and soul of all men, regardless of race, color, religion, national origin or ancestry."[7]

HOME OF THE FREE, LAND OF THE SLAVE

In declaring their independence from England, the American colonists argued that a law was void if it ran counter to a person's natural right to be free. Their belief expressed the spirit of people who had grown weary of being used by the mother country and were determined to make their way as an independent nation of free citizens. But few colonists saw fit to apply this belief to African Americans.

Slavery existed in all thirteen of the English colonies. By the beginning of the Revolutionary War, it had grown into a major business. The slave industry continued to develop in the more agricultural South, but the North also profited. Northern slave traders shipped cargoes of black people to the tobacco and rice growers in the Southern colonies and sold them at huge profits. At the same time, the Quakers were taking the lead in a moral movement against slavery. In Pennsylvania in 1775, the first Abolition Society was founded.

Many African Americans helped America win its war

for independence from England and by their participation, proved their rightful share in the victory. Slaves were hopeful that these efforts would be rewarded and after the war many submitted petitions for their freedom. Those in the South soon discovered that their hopes would not be realized. Some refused to suffer the outrage and simply escaped. But, protected by the U.S. Constitution, slavery became increasingly important as the need for labor increased throughout the South.

African-American freemen did not sit idly by. They reminded the American patriots of the African American's condition of servitude. In his "Fourth of July Oration," delivered on July 5, 1852, in Rochester, New York, Frederick Douglass said, "The rich inheritance of justice, liberty, prosperity, and independence, bequeathed by your fathers, is shared by you, not by me." And, as he later offered grim examples, "It is wrong to make men brutes, to rob them of their liberty, to work them without wages, to keep them ignorant of their relations to their fellow men, to beat them with sticks, to flay their flesh with the lash, to load their limbs with irons, to hunt them with dogs, to sell them at auction, to sunder their families, to knock out their teeth, to turn their flesh, to starve them into obedience and submission to their masters."[8] Seeking relief from this injustice, African Americans organized into little groups and assisted one another in test cases in the courts.

Eventually, the slavery issue was solved by the Civil War. But the promise and disappointment of Emancipation led African Americans to renew their protest and appeals for freedom, justice, and equality. No longer a legal issue, their freedom became a national problem and was addressed by leaders of the African-American community throughout the nation.

DAVID WALKER

WALKER'S APPEAL

David Walker (1785–1830) was a self-taught freeman from North Carolina who found conditions in his slave-holding home state intolerable. He left and worked his way to Boston, where he found employment operating a secondhand clothing store, which he eventually owned.

Although Walker had left the South, racism followed him, driving the self-made young man to express his anger and frustration in the now historic pamphlet *David Walker's Appeal, in Four Articles, Together with a Preamble, to the Colored Citizens of the World, But in Particular, and Very Expressly to Those of the United States of America*—usually called simply *Walker's Appeal*—published in Boston in 1829. The book comprised four separate articles—two addressed to whites, warning them of the consequences of their enslavement of blacks, and two to blacks, encouraging them to work at keeping their faith.

In the preamble to the four articles, Walker declares the wretchedness to which his people have been reduced as having no equal in the history of humankind and as being an affront to God and justice. Although the *Appeal* is not a speech, the Preamble seems a fitting way to introduce the speeches that follow.

MY DEARLY BELOVED BRETHREN AND FELLOW CITIZENS:

Having travelled over a considerable portion of these United States, and having, in the course of my travels taken the most accurate observations of things as they exist—the result of my observations has warranted the full and unshakened conviction, that we, (colored people of these United States) are the most degraded, wretched, and abject set of beings that ever lived since the world began, and I pray God, that none like us ever may live again until time shall be no more. They tell us of the Israelites in Egypt, the Helots in Sparta, and of the Roman Slaves, which last, were made up from almost every nation under heaven, whose sufferings under those ancient and heathen nations were, in comparison with ours, under this enlightened and christian nation, no more than a cypher—or in other words, those heathen nations of antiquity, had but little more among them than the name and form of slavery, while wretchedness and endless miseries were reserved, apparently in a phial, to be poured out upon our fathers, ourselves and our children by *christian* Americans!

These positions, I shall endeavour, by the help of the Lord, to demonstrate in the course of this *appeal,* to the satisfaction of the most incredulous mind—and may God Almighty who is the father of our Lord Jesus Christ, open your hearts to understand and believe the truth.

The *causes,* my brethren, which produce our wretchedness and miseries, are so very numerous and aggravating, that I believe the pen only of a Josephus or a Plutarch, can well enumerate and explain them. Upon subjects, then, of such incomprehensible magnitude, so impenetrable, and so notorious, I shall be obliged to omit a large class of, and content myself with giving you an exposition of a few of those, which do indeed rage to such an alarming pitch, that they cannot but be a perpetual source of terror and dismay to every reflecting mind.

I am fully aware, in making this appeal to my much afflicted and suffering brethren, that I shall not only be assailed by those whose greatest earthly desires are, to keep us in abject ignorance and wretchedness, and who are of the firm conviction that Heaven has designed us and our children to be slaves and *beasts of burden* to them and their children. I say, I do not only expect to be held up to the public as an ignorant, impudent and restless disturber of the public peace, by such avaricious creatures, as well as a mover of insubordination—and perhaps put in prison or to death, for giving a superficial exposition of our miseries, and exposing tyrants. But I am persuaded, that many of my brethren, particularly those who are ignorantly in league with slave-holders or tyrants, who acquire their daily bread by the blood and sweat of their more ignorant brethren—and not a few of those too, who are too ignorant to see an inch beyond their noses, will rise up and call me cursed—Yea, the jealous ones among us will perhaps use more abject subtlety, by affirming that this work is not worth perusing, that we are well situated, and there is no use in trying to better our condition, for we cannot. I will ask one question here.—Can our condition be any worse?—Can it be more mean and abject? If there are any changes, will they not be for the better, though they may appear for the worst at first? Can they get us any lower? Where can they get us? They are afraid to treat us worse, for they know well, the day they do it they are gone. But against all accusations which may or can be preferred against me, I appeal to Heaven for my motive in writing—who knows that my object is, if possible, to awaken in the breasts of my afflicted, degraded and slumbering brethren, a spirit of inquiry and investigation respecting our miseries and wretchedness in this REPUBLICAN LAND OF LIBERTY!!!!!!

The sources from which our miseries are derived, and on which I shall comment, I shall not combine in one, but shall put them under distinct heads and expose them in their turn; in doing which, keeping truth on my side, and not departing from the strictest rules of morality, I shall endeavour to penetrate, search out, and lay them open for your inspection. If you cannot or will not profit by them, I shall have done *my* duty to you, my country and my God.

And as the inhuman system of *slavery*, is the *source* from which most of our miseries proceed, I shall begin with that *curse to nations,* which has spread terror and devastation through so many nations of antiquity, and which is raging to such a pitch at the present day in Spain and in Portugal. It had one tug in England, in France, and in the United States of America; yet the inhabitants thereof, do not learn wisdom, and erase it entirely from their dwellings and from all with whom they have to do. The fact is, the labour of slaves comes too cheap to the avaricious usurpers, and is (as they think) of such great utility to the country where it exists, that those who are actuated by sordid avarice only, overlook the evils, which will as sure as the Lord lives, follow after the good. In fact, they are so happy to keep in ignorance and degradation, and to receive the homage and the labour of the slaves, they forget that God rules in the armies of heaven and among the inhabitants of the earth, having his ears continually open to the cries, tears and groans of his oppressed people; and being a just and holy Being will at one day appear fully in behalf of the oppressed, and arrest the progress of the avaricious oppressors; for although the destruction of the oppressors God may not effect by the oppressed, yet the Lord our God will bring other destructions upon them—for not unfrequently will he cause them to rise up one against another, to be split and divided, and to oppress each other, and sometimes to open hostilities with sword in hand.

Some may ask, what is the matter with this united and happy people?—Some say it is the cause of political usurpers, tyrants, oppressors, &c. But has not the Lord an oppressed and suffering people among them? Does the Lord condescend to hear their cries and see their tears in consequence of oppression? Will he let the oppressors rest comfortably and happy always? Will he not cause the very children of the oppressors to rise up against them, and ofttimes put them to death? "God works in many ways his wonders to perform."

I will not here speak of the destructions which the Lord brought upon Egypt, in consequence of the oppression and consequent groans of the oppressed—of the hundreds and thousands of Egyptians whom God hurled into the Red Sea for afflicting his people in their land—of the Lord's suffering people in Sparta or Lacedemon, the land of the truly famous Lycurgus—nor have I time to comment upon the cause which produced the fierceness with which Sylla usurped the title, and absolutely acted as dictator of the Roman people—the conspiracy of Cataline—the conspiracy against, and murder of Caesar in the Senate house—the spirit with which Marc Antony made himself master of the commonwealth—his associating Octavius and Lipidus with himself in power—their dividing the provinces of Rome among themselves—their attack and defeat, on the plains of Phillippi, of the last defenders of their liberty, (Brutus and Cassius)—the tyranny of Tiberius, and from him to the final overthrow of Constantinople by the Turkish Sultan, Mahomed II. A.D. 1453.

I say, I shall not take up time to speak of the *causes* which produced so much wretchedness and massacre among those heathen nations, for I am aware that you know too well, that God is just, as well as merciful!—I shall call your attention a few moments to that *Christian* nation, the Spaniards—while I shall leave almost unnoticed, that avaricious and cruel people, the Portuguese, among whom all true hearted Christians and lovers of Jesus Christ, must evidently see the judgments of God displayed. To show the judgments of God upon the Spaniards, I shall occupy but a little time, leaving a plenty of room for the candid and unprejudiced to reflect.

All persons who are acquainted with history, and particularly the Bible, who are not blinded by the God of this world, and are not actuated solely by avarice—who are able to lay aside prejudice long enough to view candidly and impartially, things as they were, are, and probably will be—who are willing to admit that God made man to serve Him *alone,* and that man should have no other Lord or Lords but Himself—that God Almighty is the *sole proprietor* or *master* of the WHOLE human family, and will not on any consideration admit of a colleague, being unwilling to divide his glory with another—and who can dispense with prejudice long enough to admit that we are *men,* notwithstanding our *improminent noses* and *woolly heads,* and believe that we feel for our fathers, mothers, wives and children, as well as the whites do for theirs.— I say, all who are permitted to see and believe these things, can easily recognize the judgments of God among the Spaniards. Though others may lay the cause of the fierceness with which they cut each other's throats, to some other circumstances, yet they who believe that God is a God of justice, will believe that SLAVERY *is the principal cause.*

While the Spaniards are running about upon the field of battle cutting each other's throats, has not the Lord an afflicted and suffering people in the midst of them, whose cries and groans in consequence of oppression are continually pouring into the ears of the God of justice? Would they not cease to cut each other's throats, if they could? But how can they? The very support which they draw from government to aid them in perpetrating such enormities, does it not arise in a great degree from the wretched victims of oppression among them? And yet they are calling for PEACE!—PEACE!! Will any peace be given unto them? Their destruction may indeed be procrastinated awhile, but can it continue long, while they are oppressing the Lord's people? Has He not the hearts of all men in His hand? Will he suffer one part of his creatures to go on oppressing another like brutes always, with impunity? And yet, those avaricious wretches are calling for PEACE!!!! I declare, it does appear to me, as though some nations think God is asleep, or that he made the Africans for nothing else but to dig their mines and work their farms, or they cannot believe history, sacred or profane.

I ask every man who has a heart, and is blessed with the privilege of believing—Is not God a God of justice to *all* his creatures? Do you say he is? Then if he gives peace and tranquillity to tyrants, and permits them to keep our fathers, our mothers, ourselves and our children in eternal ignorance and wretchedness, to support them and their families, would he be to us a God of *justice?* I ask, O ye *Christians*!!! who hold us and our children in the most abject ignorance and degradation, that ever a people were afflicted with since the world began—I say, if God gives you peace and tranquillity, and suffers you thus to go on afflicting us, and our children, who have never given you the least provocation—would he be to us *a God of justice?* If you will allow that we are MEN, who feel for each other, does not the blood of our fathers and of us their children, cry aloud to the Lord of Sabaoth against you, for the cruelties and murders with which you have, and do continue to afflict us. But it is time for me to close my remarks on the suburbs, just to enter more fully into the interior of this system of cruelty and oppression.

PETER WILLIAMS, JR.

"WE ARE NATIVES OF THIS COUNTRY"

Though it was profitable, the business of slavery had business problems. The upkeep of slave labor was expensive, not only in dollars but also in time. Slaves had to be constantly watched so that they didn't cause harm, escape, or simply waste their master's time and money.

Much of this slave unrest was inspired by the agitation of freedmen. Few of them could sit idly by while their countrymen were enslaved. Nor would they remain silent. Their voices were a constant reminder to whites that all was not well.

One solution to the problem caused by freedmen was "colonization": sending them back to Africa, thereby ridding the thirteen colonies of their "troublesome presence." The idea grew popular when those who proposed it were joined by more racist elements. Swelling the ranks of the American Colonization Society organized in 1816, these whites prepared the way for the deportation of free African Americans to Africa.

Some African Americans supported colonization.

They agreed with the Colonization Society that returning to Africa was the only way for black people to be free. But most African Americans opposed the idea, among them the Reverend Peter Williams, Jr. (1780?–1840). On July 4, 1830, he spoke at St. Phillip's Protestant Episcopal Church in New York City. He questioned the motives of those supporting colonization and declared the right of African Americans to claim America as their home. An excerpt from his speech follows.

ON THIS DAY the fathers of this nation declared, "We hold these truths to be self-evident, that all men are created equal, that they are endowed by their Creator with certain unalienable rights, among which are life, liberty, and the pursuit of happiness."

These truly noble sentiments have secured to their author a deathless fame. The sages and patriots of the Revolution subscribed them with enthusiasm and "pledged their lives, their fortunes, and their sacred honor" in their support.

The result has been the freedom and happiness of millions, by whom the annual returns of this day are celebrated with the loudest and most lively expressions of joy.

But, although this anniversary affords occasion of rejoicing to the mass of the people of the United States, there is a class, a numerous class, consisting of nearly three millions, who participate but little in its joys and are deprived of their unalienable rights by the very men who so loudly rejoice in the declaration that "all men are born free and equal."

The festivities of this day serve but to impress upon the minds of reflecting men of color a deeper sense of the cruelty, the injustice and oppression of which they have been the victims. While others rejoice in their deliverance from a foreign yoke, they mourn that a yoke a thousandfold more grievous is fastened upon them. Alas, they are slaves in the midst of freedom; they are slaves to those who boast that freedom is the unalienable right of all; and the clanking of their fetters and the voice of their wrongs make a horrid discord in the songs of freedom which resound through the land.

No people in the world profess so high a respect for liberty and equality as the people of the United States, and yet no people hold so many slaves or make such great distinctions between man and man.

From various causes . . . the work of emancipation has within a few years been rapidly advancing in a number of states. The state we live in, since the fourth of July, 1827, has been able to boast that she has no slaves, and other states where there still are slaves appear disposed to follow her example.

These things furnish us with cause of gratitude to God, and encourage us to hope that the time will speedily arrive when slavery will be universally abolished. Brethren, what a bright prospect would there be before us in this land had we no prejudices to contend against after being made free.

But, alas, the freedom to which we have attained is defective. Freedom and equality have been "put asunder." The rights of men are decided by the color of their skin; and there is as much difference made between the rights of a free white man and a free colored man as there is between a free colored man and a slave.

Though delivered from the fetters of slavery, we are oppressed by an unreasonable, unrighteous and cruel prejudice, which aims at nothing less than the forcing away of all the free colored people of the United States to the distant shores of Africa. Far be it from me to impeach the motives of every member of the African Colonization Society. The civilizing and Christianizing of that vast continent and the extirpation of the abominable traffic in slaves (which notwithstanding all the laws passed for its suppression is still carried on in all its horrors) are no doubt the principal motives which induce many to give it their support.

But there are those, and those who are most active and most influential in its cause, who hesitate not to say that they wish to rid the country of the free colored population, and there is sufficient reason to believe that with many this is the principal motive for supporting that society; and that whether Africa is civilized or not, and whether the slave trade be suppressed or not, they would wish to see the free colored people removed from this country to Africa.

Africa could certainly be brought into a state of civil and religious improvement without sending all the free people of color in the United States there.

A few well-qualified missionaries, properly fitted out and supported, would do more for the instruction and improvement of the natives of that country than a host of colonists, the greatest part of whom would need to be instructed themselves, and all of whom for a long period would find enough to do to provide for themselves instead of instructing the natives.

How inconsistent are those who say that Africa will be benefited by the removal of the free people of color of the United States there, while they say they are the *most vile and degraded* people in the world. If we are as vile and degraded as they represent us, and they wish the Africans to be rendered a virtuous, enlightened and happy people, they should not *think* of sending *us* among them, lest we should make them worse instead of better.

The colonies planted by white men on the shores of America, so far from benefiting the aborigines, corrupted their morals and caused their ruin; and yet those who say *we* are the most vile people in the world would send us to Africa to improve the character and condition of the natives. Such arguments would not be listened to for a

35

moment were not the minds of the community strangely warped by prejudice.

Those who wish that that vast continent should be *compensated* for the injuries done it, by sending thither the light of the gospel and the arts of civilized life, should aid in sending and supporting well-qualified missionaries who should be wholly devoted to the work of instruction, instead of sending colonists who would be apt to turn the ignorance of the natives to their own advantage and do them more harm than good.

Much has also been said by Colonizationists about improving the character and condition of the people of color of this country by sending them to Africa. This is more inconsistent still. We are to be improved by being sent far from civilized society. This is a novel mode of improvement. What is there in the burning sun, the arid plains, and barbarous customs of Africa, that is so peculiarly favorable to our improvement? What hinders our improving here, where schools and colleges abound, where the Gospel is preached at every corner, and where all the arts and sciences are verging fast to perfection? Nothing, nothing but prejudice. It requires no large expenditures, no hazardous enterprises to raise the people of color in the United States to as highly improved a state as any class of the community. All that is necessary is that those who profess to be anxious for it should lay aside their prejudices and act toward them as they do by others.

We are *natives* of this country, we ask only to be treated as well as *foreigners*. Not a few of our fathers suffered and bled to purchase its independence; we ask only to be treated as well as those who fought against it. We have toiled to cultivate it and to raise it to its present prosperous condition we ask only to share equal privileges with those who come from distant lands, to enjoy the fruits of our labor. Let these moderate requests be granted, and we need not go to Africa nor anywhere else to be improved and happy. We cannot but doubt the purity of the motives of those persons who deny us these requests, and would send us to Africa to gain what they might give us at home. . . .

JAMES FORTEN, SR.

"THE TEARS OF THOSE WHO WILL BE LEFT BEHIND"

First and perhaps foremost among the African Americans invited by Quakers to speak at their meetings was James Forten, Sr. (1766–1842). He had served in the Revolutionary War as a powder boy, and later trained as a sailmaker. As the owner of a sailmaking shop, he employed more than forty workers—blacks as well as whites—and became quite wealthy. Forten used his fortune and strong feelings against colonization and helped raised a force of twenty-five hundred African American volunteers to help protect a still young nation against the British in the War of 1812.

A crusader for temperance, peace, and women's rights, he worked as an organizer and wrote pamphlets in the cause for African-American progress.

The Philadelphia Female Antislavery Society invited Forten to speak as their guest on April 14, 1836. His address, most of which is printed here, stressed the need for Northern whites to continue their fight by condemning the evil of slavery practiced by their Southern neighbors.

AGAIN, THE SOUTH most earnestly and respectfully solicits the North to let the question [of] Slavery alone, and leave it to their bountiful honesty and humanity to settle. Why, honesty, I fear has fled from the South, long ago; sincerity has fallen asleep there, pity has hidden herself; justice cannot find the way; helper is not at home; charity lies dangerously ill; benevolence is under arrest; faith is nearly extinguished; truth has long since been buried, and conscience is nailed on the wall. Now, do you think it would be better to leave it to the bountiful honesty and humanity of the South to settle? No, no. Only yield to them in this one particular and they will find you vulnerable in every other.

I can tell you, my hearers, if the North once sinks into profound silence on this momentous subject, you may then bid farewell to peace, order and reform; then the condition of your fellow creatures in the southern section of our country will never be ameliorated; then may the poor slave look upon his weighty chains, and exclaim, in the agony of his heart, "To these am I immutably doomed; the glimmering rays of hope are lost to me for ever; robbed of all that is dear to man, I stand a monument of my country's ingratitude. A *husband,* yet separated from the dearest tie which binds me to this earth. A father, yet compelled to stifle the feelings of a father, and witness a helpless offspring torn by a savage hand from its mother's fond embrace, no longer to call her by that endearing title.

A wretched slave, I look upon the departing brightness of the setting sun, and when her glorious light revisits the morn, these clanking irons tell me I am that slave still; still am I to linger out a life of ignominious servitude, till death shall unloose these heavy bars—unfetter my body and soul."

You are called fanatics. Well, what if you are? Ought you to shrink from this name? God forbid. There is an eloquence in such fanaticism, for it whispers hope to the slave; there is sanctity in it, for it contains the consecrated spirit of religion; it is the fanaticism of a Benezet, a Rush, a Franklin, a Jay; the same that animated and inspired the heart of the writer of the Declaration of Independence. Then flinch not from your high duty; continue to warn the South of the awful volcano they are recklessly sleeping over; and bid them remember, too, that the drops of blood which trickle down the lacerated back of the slave, will not sink into the barren soil. No, they will rise to the common God of nature and humanity, and cry aloud for vengeance on his destroyer's head. Bid them think of this, that they may see from what quarter the terrible tempest will come; not from the breaking out of insurrections, so much dreaded, but for which men are indebted to the imagery of their minds more than to fact; not from the fanatics, or the publication of their papers, calculated to spread desolation and blood, and sever the Union, as is now basely asserted, but it will come from HIM who declared "Vengeance is mine, and I will repay."

You are not aiming to injure your southern brethren, but to benefit them; to save them from the impending storm. You are not seeking the destruction of the Union; but to render it still stronger; to link it together in one universal chain of *Justice,* and *Love,* and *Freedom.*

The Faith you have embraced teaches you to live in bonds of charity with all mankind. It is not by force of arms that Abolitionists expect to remove one of the greatest curses that ever afflicted or disgraced humanity; but by the majesty of moral power. Oh! how callous, how completely destitute of feeling, must that person be, who think of the wrongs done to the innocent and unoffending captive, and not drop one tear of pity—who can look upon slavery and not shudder at its inhuman barbarities? It is a withering blight to the country in which it exists—a deadly poison to the soil on which it is suffered to breathe—and to satiate the cravings of its appetite, it feeds, like a vulture, upon the vitals of its victims. But it is in vain that I attempt to draw a proper likeness of its horrors; it is far beyond the reach of my abilities to describe to you the endless atrocities which characterize the system. Well was it said by Thomas Jefferson, that "God has no attribute which can take sides with such oppression." See what gigantic force is concentrated in these few words—God has no attribute which can take sides with such oppression.

Ladies—I feel that I should have confined my remarks more particularly to your society, and not have extended them to the whole field of Abolition. Pardon me for the digression.

I rejoice to see you engaged in this mighty cause; it befits you; it is your province; your aid and influence is greatly to be desired in this hour of peril; it never was, never can be insignificant. Examine the records of history, and you will find that woman has been called upon in the severest trials of public emergency. That your efforts will stimulate the men to renewed exertion I have not the slightest doubt; for, in general, the pride of man's heart is such, that while he is willing to grant unto woman exclusively, many conspicuous and dignified privileges, he at the same time feels an innate disposition to check the modest ardour of her zeal and ambition, and revolts at the idea of her managing the reigns of improvement.

Therefore, you have only to be constantly exhibiting some new proof of your interest in the cause of the oppressed, and shame, if not duty, will urge our sex on the march. It has often been said by anti-abolitionists that the females have no right to interfere with the question of slavery, or petition for its overthrow; and they had better be at home attending to their domestic affairs. What a gross error—what an anti-christian spirit this bespeaks. Were not the holy commands, "Remember them that are in bonds, as bound with them," and "Do unto others as ye would they should do unto you," intended for woman to obey as well as man? Most assuredly they were.

JERMAIN WESLEY LOGUEN

"I AM A FUGITIVE SLAVE"

The Fugitive Slave Act of 1850 was created to discourage a growing number of slaves from trying to escape, and to return those who had made good their escapes. Jermain Wesley Loguen (1813–1872) was among those who had made good his escape. Loguen stole out from Tennessee to freedom on his master's horse. After working his way through college, he became a minister in Syracuse, New York. Placed at risk by the Fugitive Slave Act, Loguen publicly announced, "I am a fugitive slave from Tennessee. My master is Manasseth Loguen. The letter of the law gives him title to my person—and let him come and take it. I'll not run, nor will I give him a penny for my freedom."[9]

Speaking at a meeting in his adopted hometown of Syracuse on October 4, 1850, the Reverend Loguen cited the Fugitive Slave Act as a challenge for blacks and whites to resist the agents of this immoral law with open defiance.

I WAS A SLAVE; I knew the dangers I was exposed to. I had made up my mind as to the course I was to take. On that score I needed no counsel, nor did the colored citizens generally. They had taken their stand—they would not be taken back to slavery. If to shoot down their assailants should forfeit their lives, such result was the least of the evil. They will have their liberties or die in their defence. What is life to me if I am to be a slave in Tennessee? My neighbors! I have lived with you many years, and you know me. My home is here, and my children were born here. I am bound to Syracuse by pecuniary interests, and social and family bonds.

And do you think I can be taken away from you and from my wife and children, and be a slave in Tennessee? Has the President and his Secretary sent this enactment up here, to you, Mr. Chairman, to enforce on me in Syracuse?—and will you obey him? Did I think so meanly of you—did I suppose the people of Syracuse, strong as they are in numbers and love of liberty—or did I believe their love of liberty was so selfish, unmanly and unchristian—did I believe them so sunken and servile and degraded as to remain at their homes and labors, or, with none of that spirit which smites a tyrant down, to surround a United States Marshal to see me torn from my home and family, and hurled back to bondage—I say did I think so meanly of you, I could never come to live with you. Nor should I have stopped, on my return from Troy, twenty-four hours since, but to take my family and moveables to a neighborhood which would take fire, and arms, too, to resist the least attempt to execute this diabolical law among them.

Some kind and good friends advise me to quit my country, and stay in Canada, until this tempest is passed. I doubt not the sincerity of such counsellors. But my conviction is strong, that their advice comes from a lack of knowledge of themselves and the case in hand. I believe that their own bosoms are charged to the brim with qualities that will smite to the earth the villains who may interfere to enslave any man in Syracuse. I apprehend the advice is suggested by the perturbation of the moment, and not by the tranquil spirit that rules above the storm, in the eternal home of truth and wisdom. Therefore I have hesitated to adopt this advice, at least until I have the opinion of this meeting. Those friends have not canvassed this subject. I have. They are called suddenly to look at it. I have looked at it steadily, calmly, resolutely, and at length defiantly, for a long time.

I tell you the people of Syracuse and of the whole North must meet this tyranny and crush it by force, or be crushed by it. This hellish enactment has precipitated the conclusion that white men must live in dishonorable submission, and colored men be slaves, or they must give their physical as well as intellectual powers to the defense of human rights. The time has come to change the tones of submission into tones of defiance,—and to tell Mr. Fillmore and Mr. Webster, if they propose to execute this measure upon us, to send on their bloodhounds.

Mr. President, long ago I was beset by over-prudent and good men and women to purchase my freedom. Nay, I was frequently importuned to consent that they purchase it, and present it as evidence of their partiality to my person and character. Generous and kind as those friends were, my heart recoiled from the proposal. I owe my freedom to the God who made me, and who stirred me to claim it against all other beings in God's universe. I will not, nor will I consent, that anybody else shall countenance the claims of a vulgar despot to my soul and body. Were I in chains, and did these kind people come to buy me out of prison, I would acknowledge the boon with inexpressible thankfulness. But I feel no chains, and am in no prison. I received my freedom from Heaven, and with it came the command to defend my title to it. I have long since resolved to do nothing and suffer nothing that can, in any way, imply that I am indebted to any power but the Almighty for my manhood and personality.

Now, you are assembled here, the strength of this city is here to express their sense of this fugitive act, and to proclaim to the despots at Washington whether it shall be enforced here—whether you will permit the government to return me and other fugitives who have sought asylum among you, to the Hell of slavery. The question is with you. If you will give us up, say so, and we will shake the dust from our feet and leave you. But we believe better things. We know you are taken by surprise. The immensity of this meeting testifies to the general consternation that has brought it together, necessarily, precipitately, to decide the most stirring question that can be presented, to wit, whether, the government having transgressed Constitutional and natural limits, you will bravely resist its aggressions, and tell its soulless agents that no slave-holder shall make your city and county a hunting field for slaves.

Whatever may be your decision, my ground is taken. I have declared it everywhere. It is known over the state and out of the state—over the line in the North, and over the line in the South. I don't respect this law—I don't fear it—I won't obey it! It outlaws me, and I outlaw it, and the men who attempt to enforce it on me. I place the governmental officials on the ground that they place me. I will not live a slave, and if force is employed to reenslave me, I shall make preparations to meet the crisis as becomes a man. If you will stand by me—and I believe you will do it, for your freedom and honor are involved as well as mine—it requires no microscope to see that—I say if you will stand with us in resistance to this measure, you will be the saviors of your country. Your decision to-night in favor of resistance will give vent to the spirit of liberty, and it will break the bands of party, and shout for joy all over the North. Your example only is needed to be the

45

type of popular actions in Auburn, and Rochester, and Utica, and Buffalo, and all the West, and eventually in the Atlantic cities. Heaven knows that this act of noble daring will break out somewhere—and may God grant that Syracuse be the honored spot, whence it shall send an earthquake voice through the land!

JOHN SWEAT ROCK

"A DEEP AND CRUEL PREJUDICE"

The Civil War was fought to free the slaves, but the victory of war was short-lived. The Emancipation Proclamation did nothing to change white attitudes toward African Americans. Racial prejudice remained as strong as ever.

John Sweat Rock (1825–1866) anticipated the grim reality that ultimately came to pass. A Boston physician and attorney, the prominent professional leader wondered about the fate of free blacks in a white society.

At a meeting of the Massachusetts Anti-Slavery Society on January 23, 1862, Rock focused on the basic cause of the Civil War and debunked popular racist fears of the terrible consequences if slaves were freed. Most of that speech follows.

LADIES AND GENTLEMEN:

I am here not so much to make a speech as to add a little more *color* to this occasion.

I do not know that it is right that I should speak at

this time, for it is said that we have talked too much already; and it is being continually thundered in our ears that the time for speechmaking has ended, and the time for action has arrived. Perhaps this is so. This may be the theory of the people, but we all know that the *active* idea has found but little sympathy with either of our great military commanders or the national executive, for they have told us, again and again, that "patience is a cure for all sores," and that we must wait for the "good time," which, to us, has been long a-coming.

It is not my desire, neither is it the time for me, to criticize the government, even if I had the disposition so to do. The situation of the black man in this country is far from being an enviable one. Today, our heads are in the lion's mouth, and we must get them out the best way we can. To contend against the government is as difficult as it is to sit in Rome and fight with the pope. It is probable that, if we had the malice of the Anglo-Saxon, we would watch our chances and seize the first opportunity to take our revenge. If we attempted this, the odds would be against us, and the first thing we should know would be—*nothing*! The most of us are capable of perceiving that the man who spits against the wind spits in his own face! . . .

I do not deny that there is a deep and cruel prejudice lurking in the bosoms of the white people of this country. It is much more abundant in the North than in the South. Here, it is to be found chiefly among the higher and lower classes; and there is no scarcity of it among the poor whites at the South.

The cause of this prejudice may be seen at a glance. The educated and wealthy class despise the Negro because they have robbed him of his hard earnings or, at least, have got rich off the fruits of his labor; and they believe if he gets his freedom, their fountain will be dried up, and they will be obliged to seek business in a new channel. Their "occupation will be gone." The lowest class hate him because he is poor, as they are, and is a competitor with them for the same labor. The poor, ignorant white man, who does not understand that the interest of the laboring classes is mutual, argues in this wise: "Here is so much labor to be performed, that darkey does it. If he was gone, I should have his place." The rich and the poor are both prejudiced from interest, and not because they entertain vague notions of justice and humanity.

While uttering my solemn protest against this American vice, which has done more than any other thing to degrade the American people in the eyes of the civilized world, I am happy to state that there are many who have never known this sin, and many others who have been converted to the truth by the "foolishness of anti-slavery preaching," and are deeply interested in the welfare of the race, and never hesitate to use their means and their influence to help break off the yoke that has been so long crushing us. I thank them all and hope the number may be multiplied, until we shall have a people who will know no man save by his virtues and his merits.

Now, it seems to me that a blind man can see that the present war is an effort to nationalize, perpetuate, and extend slavery in this country. In short, slavery is the cause of the war: I might say, is *the* war itself. Had it not been for slavery, we should have had no war! Through 240 years of indescribable tortures, slavery has wrung out of the blood, bones, and muscles of the Negro hundreds of millions of dollars and helped much to make this nation rich. At the same time, it has developed a volcano which has burst forth, and, in a less number of days than years, has dissipated this wealth and rendered the government bankrupt! And, strange as it may appear, you still cling to this monstrous iniquity, notwithstanding it is daily sinking the country lower and lower! Some of our ablest and best men have been sacrificed to appease the wrath of this American god.

The government wishes to bring back the country to

what it was before. This is possible; but what is to be gained by it? If we are fools enough to retain the cancer that is eating out our vitals, when we can safely extirpate it, who will pity us if we see our mistake when we are past recovery? The Abolitionists saw this day of tribulation and reign of terror long ago, and warned you of it; *but you would not hear*! You now say that it is their agitation which has brought about this terrible civil war! That is to say, your friend sees a slow match set near a keg of gunpowder in your house and timely warns you of the danger which he sees is inevitable; you despise his warning, and, after the explosion, say, if he had not told you of it, it would not have happened!

Now, when some leading men who hold with the policy of the President, and yet pretend to be liberal, argue that while they are willing to admit that the slave has an undoubted right to his liberty, the master has an equal right to his property; that to liberate the slave would be to injure the master, and a greater good would be accomplished to the country in these times by the loyal master's retaining his property than by giving to the slave his liberty—I do not understand it so. Slavery is treason against God, man, and the nation. The master has no right to be a partner in a conspiracy which has shaken the very foundation of the government. Even to apologize for it, while in open rebellion, is to aid and abet in treason.

The master's right to his property in human flesh cannot be equal to the slave's right to his liberty. The former right is acquired, either by kidnapping or unlawful purchase from kidnapers, or inheritance from kidnapers. The very claim invalidates itself. On the other hand, liberty is the inalienable right of every human being; and liberty can make no compromise with slavery.

Today, when it is a military necessity, and when the safety of the country is dependent upon emancipation, our humane political philosophers are puzzled to know what would become of the slaves if they were emancipated! The idea seems to prevail that the poor things would suffer if robbed of the glorious privileges that they now enjoy! If they could not be flogged, half starved, and work to support in ease and luxury those who have never waived an opportunity to outrage and wrong them, they would pine away and die! Do you imagine that the Negro can live outside of slavery? Of course, now, they can take care of themselves and their masters too; but if you give them their liberty, must they not suffer?

Have you never been able to see through all this? Have you not observed that the location of this organ of sympathy is in the pocket of the slaveholder and the man who shares in the profits of slave labor? Of course you have; and pity those men who have lived upon their ill-gotten wealth. You know, if they do not have somebody to work for them, they must leave their gilded *salons*, and take off their coats and roll up their sleeves, and take their chances among the *live* men of the world. This, you are aware, these respectable gentlemen will not do, for they have been so long accustomed to live by robbing and cheating the Negro that they are sworn never to work while they can live by plunder. . . .

EMANCIPATION AND RECONSTRUCTION

President Abraham Lincoln issued the Emancipation Proclamation in 1863, two years before the Union victory in the Civil War. The Thirteenth (1865), Fourteenth (1866), and Fifteenth (1868) Amendments to the Constitution were enacted after the Civil War. At long last, the freedoms and rights of white American men—at least on paper—were extended to black Americans.

None of these measures prevented whites, especially in the South, from doing all they could to set back the clock. During the Reconstruction period that followed the Civil War, defeated white Confederates tried to rebuild a destroyed South and restore themselves to their former privilege and power. Between 1866 and 1879, white mobs murdered more than three thousand African Americans. White-controlled Southern state legislatures passed Black Codes restricting black rights and eliminating the black franchise. Fear of white terror forced many thousands of blacks to migrate west and north.

Yet if Reconstruction saw the return of oppression,

the period was also a time to win back what blacks had lost. African Americans began organizing into protest organizations to agitate, conduct nationwide conventions, examine national problems, and create coordinated forms of economic, educational, and political action. African Americans slowly began to realize that in unity there was strength.

By the turn of the century, black people had formed African-American Councils, Pan-African Conventions, and National Equal Rights Leagues. From those and other national organizations would emerge the National Association for the Advancement of Colored People and the Urban League, which would lead to the creation of the modern civil rights movement.

SOJOURNER TRUTH

"I WANT WOMEN TO HAVE THEIR RIGHTS.... I WILL SHAKE EVERY PLACE I GO TO"

Sojourner Truth (1797?–1883) was born to a Dutch-speaking family about 1797. The eleventh child in her family, she remained a slave in upstate New York until 1827. She was then freed under the state's gradual emancipation act. Two years later she moved to New York City, where for a time she was a member of a religious cult. The cult did not last long, but the religious feeling she experienced grew into a calling that guided her across the land, preaching and lecturing on freedom for her people. Not content simply to speak, Sojourner Truth became an antislavery activist and helped slaves settle themselves in the North during the Civil War.

Of special interest in all her talks in the years following emancipation were the rights of women, for which she spoke out even when she was in her eighties. At the first annual meeting of the American Equal Rights Association in New York City, May 9 and 10, 1867, she cited the disadvantages of being a woman of color in a racist and sexist society and called on all women to join with men in the fight for equality. Part of her speech follows.

MY FRIENDS, I am rejoiced that you are glad, but I don't know how you will feel when I get through.

I come from another field—the country of the slave. They have got their rights—so much good luck. Now what is to be done about it? I feel that I have got as much responsibility as anybody else. I have as good rights as anybody.

There is a great stir about colored men getting their rights, but not a word about the colored women; and if colored men get their rights, and not colored women get theirs, there will be a bad time about it. So I am for keeping the thing going while things are stirring; because if we wait till it is still, it will take a great while to get it going again. White women are a great deal smarter, and know more than colored women, while colored women do not know scarcely anything. They go out washing, which is about as high as a colored woman gets, and their men go about idle, strutting up and down; and when the women come home, they ask for their money and take it all, and then scold because there is no food. I want you to consider on that, chil'n. I want women to have their rights.

In the courts women have no right, no voice; nobody speaks for them. I wish woman to have her voice there among the pettifoggers. If it is not a fit place for women, it is unfit for men to be there. I am above eighty years old; it is about time for me to be going. But I suppose I am kept here because something remains for me to do; I suppose I am yet to help break the chain. I have done a great deal of work—as much as a man, but did not get so much pay. I used to work in the field and bind grain, keeping up with the cradler; but men never doing no more, got twice as much pay. So with the German women. They work in the field and do as much work, but do not get the pay. We do as much, we eat as much, we want as much.

I suppose I am about the only colored woman that goes about to speak for the rights of the colored woman, I want to keep the thing stirring, now that the ice is broken. What we want is a little money. You men know that you get as much again as women when you write, or for what you do. When we get our rights, we shall not have to come to you for money, for then we shall have money enough of our own. It is a good consolation to know that when we have got this we shall not be coming to you any more.

You have been having our right so long, that you think, like a slaveholder, that you own us. I know that it is hard for one who has held the reins for so long to give up; it cuts like a knife. It will feel all better when it closes up again. I have been in Washington about three years, seeing about those colored people. Now colored men have a right to vote; and what I want is to have colored women have the right to vote. There ought to be equal rights more than ever, since colored people have got their freedom.

I know that it is hard for men to give up entirely. They must run in the old track. I was amused how men speak up for one another. They cannot bear that a woman should say anything about the man, but they will stand here and take up the time in man's cause. But we are going, tremble or no tremble. Men are trying to help us. I know that all—the spirit they have got; and they cannot help us much until some of the spirit is taken out of them that belongs among the women. Men have got their rights, and women has not got their rights. That is the trouble. When woman gets her rights man will be right. How beautiful that will be. Then it will be peace on earth and good will to men. . . .

And now when the waters is troubled, and now is the time to step into the pool. There is a great deal now with the minds, and now is the time to start forth. . . . The great fight was to keep the rights of the poor colored people. That made a great battle. And now I hope that this will be the last battle that will be in the world. Let us finish up so that there be no more fighting. I have faith in God and there is truth in humanity. Be strong women! Blush not! Tremble not! I want you to keep a good faith and good courage. And I am going round after I get my business settled and get more equality. People in the North, I am going round to lecture on human rights. I will shake every place I go to.

ROBERT B. ELLIOTT

"MARKED WAS THEIR VALOR"

Robert B. Elliott (1842–1884) was born of West Indian immigrants in Boston. He studied law abroad under a London barrister. Upon his return to the United States, he settled in South Carolina and became one of twenty-two African Americans to serve in Congress during Reconstruction.

Elliott's last term in Congress was highlighted by his eloquent support of a civil rights bill designed to secure equality for and prohibit discrimination against African Americans in all public places. "The Constitution warrants it; the Supreme Court sanctions it; justice demands it," Elliott declared in a speech before Congress on January 6, 1874. The following is excerpted from that speech.

MR. SPEAKER: While I am sincerely grateful for this high mark of courtesy that have been accorded to me by this House, it is a matter of regret to me that it is necessary at this day that I should rise in the presence of an American Congress to advocate a bill which simply asserts equal rights and equal public privileges for all classes of American citizens. I regret, sir, that the dark hue of my skin may lend a color to the imputation that I am controlled by motives personal to myself in my advocacy of this great measure of national justice. Sir, the motive that impels me is restricted by no such narrow boundary, but is as broad as your Constitution. I advocate it, sir, because it is right. The bill, however, not only appeals to your justice, but it demands a response from your gratitude.

In the events that led to the achievement of American independence the Negro was not an inactive or unconcerned spectator. He bore his part bravely upon many battlefields, although uncheered by that certain hope of political elevation which victory would secure to the white man. The tall granite shaft, which a grateful State has reared above its sons who fell in defending Fort Griswold against the attack of Benedict Arnold, bears the name of Jordan, Freeman, and other brave men of the African race, who there cemented with their blood the cornerstone of the Republic. In the state which I have the honor in part to represent (South Carolina) the rifle of the black man rang out against the troops of the British Crown in the darkest days of the American Revolution. Said General Greene, who has been justly termed the "Washington of the North," in a letter written by him to Alexander Hamilton, on the tenth of January, 1781, from the vicinity of Camden, South Carolina:

> "There is no such thing as national character or national sentiment. The inhabitants are numerous, but they would be rather formidable abroad than at home. There is a great spirit of enterprise among the black people, and those that come out as volunteers are not a little formidable to the enemy."

At the battle of New Orleans under the immortal Jackson, a colored regiment held the extreme right of the American line unflinchingly and drove back the British column that pressed upon them at the point of the bayonet. So marked was their valor on that occasion that it evoked from their great commander the warmest encomiums, as will be seen from his dispatch announcing the brilliant victory.

As the gentleman from Kentucky (Mr. Beck), who seems to be the leading exponent on this floor of the party that is arrayed against the principle of this bill, has been pleased, in season and out of season, to cast odium upon the Negro and to vaunt the chivalry of his state, I may be pardoned for calling attention to another portion of the same dispatch. Referring to the various regiments under his command, and their conduct on that field which terminated the second war of American Independence, General Jackson says,

"At the very moment when the entire discomfiture of the enemy was looked for with a confidence amounting to certainty, the Kentucky reinforcements, in whom so much reliance had been placed, ingloriously fled."

In quoting this indisputable piece of history, I do so only by way of admonition and not to question the well-attested gallantry of the true Kentuckian, and to the gentleman that it would be well that he should not flaunt his heraldry so proudly while he bears this bar sinister on the military escutcheon of his state—a state which answered the call of the Republic in 1861, when treason thundered at the very gates of the Capital, by coldly declaring her neutrality in the impending struggle. The Negro, true to that patriotism and love of country that have ever marked and characterized his history on this continent, came to the aid of the government in its efforts to maintain the Constitution. To that government he now appeals; that Constitution he now invokes for protection against outrage and unjust prejudices founded upon caste.

BLANCHE KELSO BRUCE

"WE ARE DETERMINED"

During Reconstruction, African Americans experienced their first and fullest measure of political opportunities. Many took advantage and gained political offices. None succeeded more fully than Blanche Kelso Bruce (1841–1898), who was born in Virginia, and later attended Oberlin College in Ohio. After two years, Bruce moved to Mississippi, where he was elected to various state offices and eventually, in 1874, to the United States Senate.

Bruce spent a good deal of his time fighting for civil rights in the South, and he was always cognizant of his enemies—those determined to undo the recent gains made by African Americans. As he explained in a speech to the Senate on March 31, 1876, and excerpted below, "We do not ask the enactment of new laws, but only the enforcement of those that already exist."

WE WANT PEACE and good order at the South. But it can only come by the fullest recognition of the rights of all classes. The opposition must concede the necessity of change, not only in the temper but in the philosophy of their party organization and management. The sober American judgment must obtain in the South as elsewhere in the republic, that the only distinctions upon which parties can be safely organized and in harmony with our institutions are differences of opinions relative to principles and policy of government, and that differences of religion, nationality, or race can neither with safety nor propriety be permitted for a moment to enter into the party contests of the day.

The unanimity with which the colored voters act with a party is not referable to any race prejudice on their part. On the contrary, they invite the political cooperation of their white brethren, and vote as a unit because proscribed as such. They deprecate the establishment of the color line by the opposition, not only because the act is unwise and wrong in principle but because it isolates them from the white men of the South, and forces them, in sheer self-protection and against their inclination, to act seemingly upon the basis of a race prejudice that they neither respect nor entertain.

As a class they are free from prejudices and have no uncharitable suspicions against their white fellow citizens, whether native-born or settlers from the Northern states. They not only recognize the equality of citizenship and the right of every man to hold, without proscription, any position of honor and trust to which the confidence of the people may elevate him but, owing nothing to race, birth, or surroundings, they, above all other classes in the community, are interested to see prejudices drop out of both politics and the business of the country, and success in life proceed only upon the integrity and merit of the man who seeks it. They are also appreciative—feeling and exhibiting the liveliest gratitude for counsel and help in their new career, whether they come from the men of the North or of the South.

But withal, as they progress in intelligence and appreciation of the dignity of their prerogatives as citizens, they, as an evidence of growth, begin to realize the significance of the proverb, "When thou doest well for thyself, men shall praise thee": and are disposed to exact the same protection and concession of rights that are conferred upon other citizens by the Constitution, and that, too, without the humiliation involved in the enforced abandonment of their political convictions.

We simply demand the practical recognition of the rights given us in the Constitution and laws, and ask from our white fellow citizens only the consideration and fairness that we so willingly extend to them. Let them generally realize and concede that citizenship imports to us what it does to them, no more and no less, and impress the colored people that a party defeat does not imperil their political franchise. Let them cease their attempts to coerce our political cooperation, and invite and secure it by a policy so fair and just as to commend itself to our judgment, and resort to no motive or measure to control us that self-respect would preclude their applying to themselves. When we can entertain opinions and select party affiliations without proscription, and cast our ballots as other citizens and without jeopardy to person or privilege, we can safely afford to be governed by the considerations that ordinarily determine the political action of American citizens.

But we must be guaranteed in the unproscribed exercise of our honest convictions and be absolutely, from within or without, protected in the use of our ballot before we can either wisely or safely decide our vote. In union, not division, is strength, so long as White League proscription renders division of our vote impracticable by making a difference of opinion opprobrious and an antagonism in politics a crime. On the other hand, if we should, from considerations of fear, yield to the shotgun policy of our opponents, the White League might win a temporary success, but the ultimate result would be disastrous to both races, for they would first become aggressively turbulent, and we, as a class, would become servile, unreliable, and worthless.

It has been suggested, as the popular sentiment of the country, that the colored citizens must no longer expect special legislation for their benefit, nor exceptional interference by the national government for their protection. If this is true, if such is the judgment relative to our demands and needs, I venture to offset the suggestion, so far as it may be used as reason for a denial of the protection we seek, by the statement of another and more prevalent popular conviction. Back of this, and underlying the foundations of the republic itself, there lies deep in the breasts of the patriotic millions of the country the conviction that the laws must be enforced, and life, liberty, and property must, alike to all and for all, be protected. But I allege that we do not seek special action in our behalf, except to meet special danger, and only then such as all classes of citizens are entitled to receive under the Constitution. We do not ask the enactment of new laws, but only the enforcement of those that already exist.

The vicious and exceptional political action had by the White League in Mississippi has been repeated in other contests and in other states of the South, and the colored voters have been subjected therein to outrages upon their rights similar to those perpetrated in my own state at the recent election. Because violence has become so general a quality in the political canvasses of the South and my people the common sufferers in each instance, I have considered this subject more in detail than would, under other circumstances, have been either appropriate or necessary. As the proscription and violence toward the colored voters are special and almost exclusive, and seem to proceed upon the assumption that there is something exceptionally offensive and unworthy in them, I have felt, as the only representative of my race in the Senate of the

United States, that I was placed, in some sort, upon the defensive; and I have consequently endeavored to show how aggravated and inexcusable were the wrongs worked upon us, and have sought to vindicate our title to both the respect and goodwill of the just people of the nation.

The gravity of the issues involved has demanded great plainness of speech from me. But I have endeavored to present my views to the Senate with the moderation and deference inspired by the recollection that both my race and myself were once bondsmen, and are today debtors largely to the love and justice of a great people for the enjoyment of our personal and political liberty. While my antecedents and surroundings suggest modesty, there are some considerations that justify frankness, and even boldness of speech. . . .

I have confidence, not only in my country and her institutions but in the endurance, capacity, and destiny of my people. We will, as opportunity offers and ability serves, seek our places, sometimes in the field of letters, arts, sciences, and the professions. More frequently mechanical pursuits will attract and elicit our efforts; more still of my people will find employment and livelihood as the cultivators of the soil. The bulk of this people—by surroundings, habits, adaptation, and choice—will continue to find their homes in the South and constitute the masses of its yeomanry. We will there, probably, of our own volition and more abundantly than in the past, produce the great staples that will contribute to the basis of foreign exchange, aid in giving the nation a balance of trade, and minister to the wants and comfort and build up the prosperity of the whole land.

Whatever our ultimate position in the composite civilization of the republic and whatever varying fortunes attend our career, we will not forget our instincts for freedom nor our love of country. Guided and guarded by a beneficent Providence, and living under the genial influence of liberal institutions, we have no apprehensions that we shall fail from the land from attrition with other races, or ignobly disappear from either the politics or industries of the country.

Mr. President, allow me here to say that, although many of us are uneducated in the schools, we are informed and advised as to our duties to the government, our state, and ourselves. Without class prejudice or animosities, with obedience to authority as the lesson and love of peace and order as the passion of our lives, with scrupulous respect for the rights of others, and with the hopefulness of political youth, we are determined that the great government that gave us liberty and rendered its gift valuable by giving us the ballot shall not find us wanting in a sufficient response to any demand that humanity or patriotism may make upon us; and we ask such action as will not only protect us in the enjoyment of our constitutional rights but will preserve the integrity of our republican institutions.

FREDERICK DOUGLASS

"WHO WOULD BE FREE, THEMSELVES MUST STRIKE THE BLOW"

He was often called "the unofficial president of American Negroes." In the years before and immediately after the Civil War, no one was to represent the hearts and minds of African-American people or disturb whites of opposing views more than Frederick Douglass (1817–1895).

Foremost among African-American abolitionists, Douglass believed that he and other African Americans could contribute most by being politically active in the antislavery movement.

Douglass wrote and spoke at every opportunity about the need for African-American freedom. Seeing the promise of politics as the most effective way to achieve this goal, he became a political force. As keynote speaker at the Louisville Convention in Kentucky, September 24, 1883, he spoke to the needs of all Americans—all those with a stake in improved race relations—at a time the Republican party was discarding the issues on which it had based its Reconstruction policies.

In this speech, excerpted below, Douglass stressed the

commonality between the races in their allegiance to, and aspirations for, the nation. He lamented the conspiracy against African Americans for achieving their just desserts and laid the blame squarely on a government of unconscionable whites.

WITH APPARENT SURPRISE, astonishment and impatience we have been asked: "What more can the colored people of this country want than they now have, and what more is possible to them?" It is said they were once slaves, they are now free; they were once subjects, they are now sovereigns; they were once outside of all American institutions, they are now inside of all and are a recognized part of the whole American people. Why, then, do they hold Colored National Conventions and thus insist upon keeping up the color line between themselves and their white fellow countrymen? We do not deny the pertinence and plausibility of these questions, nor do we shrink from a candid answer to the argument which they are supposed to contain. For we do not forget that they are not only put to us by those who have no sympathy with us, but by many who wish us well, and that in any case they deserve an answer.

Before, however, we proceed to answer them, we digress here to say that there is only one element associated with them which excites the least bitterness of feeling in us or that calls for special rebuke, and that is when they fall from the lips and pens of colored men who suffer with us and ought to know better. A few such men, well known to us and the country, happening to be more fortunate in the possession of wealth, education and position than their humbler brethren, have found it convenient to chime in with the popular cry against our assembling, on the ground that we have no valid reason for this measure or for any other separate from the whites; that we ought to be satisfied with things as they are.

With white men who thus object the case is different

69

and less painful. For them there is a chance for charity. Educated as they are and have been for centuries, taught to look upon colored people as a lower order of humanity than themselves and as having few rights, if any, above domestic animals, regarding them also through the medium of their beneficent religious creeds and just laws— as if law and practice were identical—some allowance can, and perhaps ought to, be made when they misapprehend our real situation and deny our wants and assume a virtue they do not possess.

But no such excuse or apology can be properly framed for men who are in any way identified with us. What may be erroneous in others implies either baseness or imbecility in them. Such men, it seems to us, are either deficient in self-respect or too mean, servile and cowardly to assert the true dignity of their manhood and that of their race. To admit that there are such men among us is a disagreeable and humiliating confession. But in this respect, as in others, we are not without the consolation of company: we are neither alone nor singular in the production of just such characters. All oppressed people have been thus afflicted.

It is one of the most conspicuous evils of caste and oppression, that they inevitably tend to make cowards and serviles of their victims, men ever ready to bend the knee to pride and power that thrift may follow fawning, willing to betray the cause of the many to serve the ends of the few; men who never hesitate to sell a friend when they think they can thereby purchase an enemy. Specimens of this sort may be found everywhere and at all times. There were Northern men with Southern principles in the time of slavery, and Tories in the revolution for independence.

There are betrayers and informers today in Ireland, ready to kiss the hand that smites them and strike down the arm reached out to save them. Considering our long subjection to servitude and caste, and the many temptations to which we are exposed to betray our race into the hands of their enemies, the wonder is not that we have so many traitors among us as that we have so few.

The most of our people, to their honor be it said, are remarkably sound and true to each other.

If liberty, with us, is yet but a name, our citizenship is but a sham, and our suffrage thus far only a cruel mockery, we may yet congratulate ourselves upon the fact, that the laws and institutions of the country are sound, just and liberal. There is hope for a people when their laws are righteous, whether for the moment they conform to their requirements or not. But until this nation shall make its practice accord with its Constitution and its righteous laws, it will not do to reproach the colored people of this country with keeping up the color line—for that people would prove themselves scarcely worthy of even theoretical freedom, to say nothing of practical freedom, if they settled down in silent, servile and cowardly submission to their wrongs, from fear of making their color visible. They are bound by every element of manhood to hold conventions, in their own name, and on their own behalf, to keep their grievances before the people and make every organized protest against the wrongs inflicted upon them within their power. They should scorn the counsels of cowards, and hang their banner on the outer wall.

Who would be free, themselves must strike the blow. We do not believe, as we are often told, that the Negro is the ugly child of the National family, and the more he is kept out of sight the better it will be for him. You know that liberty given is never so precious as liberty sought for and fought for. The man outraged is the man to make the outcry. Depend upon it, men will not care much for a people who do not care for themselves.

Our meeting here was opposed by some of our members, because it would disturb the peace of the Republican party. The suggestion came from coward lips and misapprehended the character of that party. If the Republican party cannot stand a demand for justice and fair play, it ought to go down. We were men before that party was born, and our manhood is more sacred than any party can be. Parties were made for men, not men for parties.

If the six millions of colored people of this country, armed with the Constitution of the United States, with a million votes of their own to lean upon, and millions of white men at their back, whose hearts are responsive to the claims of humanity, have not sufficient spirit and wisdom to organize and combine to defend themselves from outrage, discrimination and oppression, it will be idle for them to expect that the Republican party or any other political party will organize and combine for them or care what becomes of them. Men may combine to prevent cruelty to animals, for they are dumb and cannot speak for themselves; but we are men and must speak for ourselves, or we shall not be spoken for at all.

We have conventions in America for Ireland, but we should have none if Ireland did not speak for herself. It is because she makes a noise and keeps her cause before the people that other people go to her help. It was the sword of Washington that gave Independence the sword of Lafayette.

In conclusion upon this color objection, we have to say that we meet here in open daylight. There is nothing sinister about us. The eyes of the nation are upon us. Ten thousand newspapers may tell if they choose of whatever is said and done here. They may commend our wisdom or condemn our folly, precisely as we shall be wise or foolish. We put ourselves before them as honest men and ask their judgment upon our work. . . .

MARY CHURCH TERRELL

"THE PROGRESS OF COLORED WOMEN"

Mary Church Terrell (1863–1954) was the first president of the National Association of Colored Women, which she helped found in 1896. The honor was a tribute to a woman who led the fight for civil rights for African Americans and for the right of women to vote.

The national organization she headed was composed of black women's clubs throughout the nation and helped improve the lives of countless black people when there was nowhere else for them to turn.

Invited to speak at the Congressional Association of Maryland and the District of Columbia in 1904, Mary Terrell reported on "The Progress of Colored Women." In that speech, excerpted below, she praised their virtues and accomplishments while recognizing the numerous prejudices they had to overcome. Her remarks were published in *The Voice of the Negro* in July 1904.

WHEN ONE CONSIDERS the obstacles encountered by colored women in their effort to educate and cultivate themselves, since they became free, the work they have accomplished and the progress they have made will bear favorable comparison, at least with that of their more fortunate sisters, from whom the opportunity of acquiring knowledge and the means of self-culture have never been entirely withheld. Not only are colored women with ambition and aspiration handicapped on account of their sex, but they are almost everywhere baffled and mocked because of their race. Not only because they are women, but because they are colored women are discouragement and disappointment meeting them at every turn.

But in spite of the obstacles encountered, the progress made by colored women along many lines appears like a veritable miracle of modern times. Forty years ago for the great masses of colored women there was no such thing as home. Today in each and every section of the country there are hundreds of homes among colored people, the mental and moral tone of which is as high and as pure as can be found among the best people of any land.

To the women of the race may be attributed in large measure the refinement and purity of the colored home. The immorality of colored women is a theme upon which those who know little about them or those who maliciously misrepresent them love to descant. Foul aspersions upon the character of colored women are assiduously circulated by the press of certain sections and especially by the direct descendants of those who in years past were responsible for the moral degradation of their female slaves.

And yet, in spite of the fateful heritage of slavery, even though the safeguards usually thrown around maidenly youth and innocence are in some sections entirely withheld from colored girls, statistics compiled by men not inclined to falsify in favor of my race show that immorality among the colored women of the United States is not so great as among women with similar environment and temptations in Italy, Germany, Sweden and France.

Scandals in the best colored society are exceedingly rare, while the progressive game of divorce and remarriage is practically unknown.

The intellectual progress of colored women has been marvelous. So great has been their thirst for knowledge and so Herculean their efforts to acquire it that there are few colleges, universities, high and normal schools in the North, East and West from which colored girls have not graduated with honor. In Wellesley, Vassar, Ann Arbor, Cornell and in Oberlin, my dear alma mater, whose name will always be loved and whose praise will always be sung as the first college in the country broad, just and generous enough to extend a cordial welcome to the Negro and to open its doors to women on an equal footing with the men, colored girls by their splendid records have forever settled the question of their capacity and worth. The instructors in these and other institutions cheerfully bear testimony to their intelligence, their diligence and their success.

As the brains of colored women expanded, their hearts began to grow. No sooner had the heads of a favored few been filled with knowledge than their hearts yearned to dispense blessings to the less fortunate of their race. With tireless energy and eager zeal, colored women have worked in every conceivable way to elevate their race. Of the colored teachers engaged in instructing our youth it is probably no exaggeration to say that fully eighty percent are women. In the backwoods, remote from the civilization and comforts of the city and town colored women may be found courageously battling with those evils which such conditions always entail. Many a heroine of whom the world will never hear has thus sacrificed her life to her race amid surroundings and in the face of privations which only martyrs can bear. . . .

It is almost impossible to ascertain exactly what the Negro is doing in any field, for the records are so poorly kept. This is particularly true in the case of the women of the race. During the past forty years there is no doubt that colored women in their poverty have contributed large sums of money to charitable and educational institutions as well as to the foreign and home missionary work. Within the twenty-five years in which the educational work of the African Methodist Episcopal Church has been systematized, the women of that organization have contributed at least five hundred thousand dollars to the cause of education. Dotted all over the country are charitable institutions for the aged, orphaned and poor which have been established by colored women. Just how many it is difficult to state, owing to the lack of statistics bearing on the progress, possessions and prowess of colored women. . . .

Up to date, politics have been religiously eschewed by colored women, although questions affecting our legal status as a race is sometimes agitated by the most progressive class. In Louisiana and Tennessee colored women have several times petitioned the legislatures of their respective states to repel the obnoxious Jim-Crow-car laws. Against the convict-lease system, whose atrocities have been so frequently exposed of late, colored women here and there in the South are waging a ceaseless war. So long as hundreds of their brothers and sisters, many of whom have committed no crime or misdemeanor whatever, are thrown into cells whose cubic contents are less than those of a goodsize grave, to be overworked, underfed and only partially covered with vermin-infested rags, and so long as children are born to the women in these camps who breathe the polluted atmosphere of these dens of horror and vice from the time they utter their first cry in the world till they are released from their suffering by death, colored women who are working for the emancipation and elevation of their race know where their duty lies. By constant agitation of this painful and hideous subject they hope to touch the conscience of the country, so that this stain upon its escutcheon shall be forever wiped away.

Alarmed at the rapidity with which the Negro is losing ground in the world of trade, some of the farsighted women are trying to solve the labor question, so far as it concerns the women at least, by urging the establishment of schools of domestic science wherever means therefor can be secured. Those who are interested in this particular work hope and believe that if colored women and girls are thoroughly trained in domestic service, the boycott which has undoubtedly been placed upon them in many sections of the country will be removed. With so few vocations open to the Negro and with the labor organizations increasingly hostile to him, the future of the boys and girls of the race appears to some of our women very foreboding and dark.

The cause of temperance has been eloquently espoused by two women, each of whom has been appointed national superintendent of work among colored people by the Woman's Christian Temperance Union. In business, colored women have had signal success. There is in Alabama a large milling and cotton business belonging to and controlled by a colored woman, who has sometimes as many as seventy-five men in her employ. Until a few years ago the principal ice plant of Nova Scotia was owned and managed by a colored woman, who sold it for a large amount. In the professions there are dentists and doctors whose practice is lucrative and large. Ever since a book was published in 1773 entitled "Poems on Various Subjects, Religious and Moral by Phillis Wheatley, Negro Servant of Mr. John Wheatley," of Boston, colored women have given abundant evidence of literary ability. In sculpture we are represented by a woman upon whose chisel Italy has set her seal of approval; in painting by one of Bouguereau's pupils and in music by young women holding diplomas from the best conservatories in the land.

In short, to use a thought of the illustrious Frederick Douglass, if judged by the depths from which they have come, rather than by the heights to which those blessed with centuries of opportunities have attained, colored women need not hang their heads in shame. They are slowly but surely making their way up to the heights, wherever they can be scaled. In spite of handicaps and discouragements they are not losing heart. In a variety of ways they are rendering valiant service to their race. Lifting as they climb, onward and upward they go struggling and striving and hoping that the buds and blossoms of their desires may burst into glorious fruition ere long. Seeking no favors because of their color nor charity because of their needs they knock at the door of Justice and ask for an equal chance.

III

RENEWED RACIAL STRATEGIES

By the turn of the twentieth century, African Americans began to realize that if their conditions were ever to improve, it was going to be up to them. To "cast down your bucket where you are" or to follow the migration of white Americans into the cities of the North were two alternatives and personal decisions they had to make.

But the choice turned out to be more geographical than social. Segregation and discrimination continued to rule black lives, and the crime of racial lynchings remained. Between 1900 and 1920, nearly two thousand African Americans lost their lives to mob violence. Southern whites finding a black person whom they could blame for misconduct took justice into their own hands.

In this climate of racial terror, African-American organizations, increased in number and influence. The National Urban League and the National Association for the Advancement of Colored People, two of the earliest and most influential of African-American organizations working for the social betterment of minorities, were joined by hundreds of other organizations.

The service record of African Americans in two world wars did nothing to relieve their oppression. As members of the U.S. military, 370,000 African Americans (eleven percent of American combat forces) served in World War I, about one million, including several thousand women, in World War II. All fought in segregated branches of the service, and few enjoyed the rewards of peace. Whereas race riots followed one war, race prejudice continued after the other. The time had passed for African Americans to wait for their civil rights. It was time for them to demand their rights with renewed determination.

BOOKER T. WASHINGTON

"THE FRIENDSHIP OF THE TWO RACES"

The most famous black leader of his generation, Booker T. Washington (1856–1915) was a moderate who believed that civil rights meant civil responsibility. He felt that African Americans should forget about civil rights legislation in the South and win dignity and respect through self-help and self-improvement. It was an opinion that he lived by, angering black militants and intellectuals and dividing black Americans.

Washington was born a slave on a plantation in Virginia. After attending elementary school for "colored" children, he set out, at the age of seventeen, for Hampton Institute in Norfolk, Virginia. Three years later, he was chosen by the principal to head a school being started in Tuskegee, Alabama, to specialize in industrial education for black students. Washington built Tuskegee into one of the most important black colleges in America.

Because of Washington's efforts, thousands of African-American students were able to gain an education they would otherwise have been denied. His success as an educator and leader earned him national recognition. But he is most remembered for his philosophy of racial accommodation. His speech, excerpted below, at the Cotton States and International Exposition in Atlanta, Georgia, September 18, 1895, was the major presentation of this philosophy.

MR. PRESIDENT AND GENTLEMEN OF THE BOARD OF DIRECTORS AND CITIZENS:

One-third of the population of the South is of the Negro race. No enterprise seeking the material, civil, or moral welfare of this section can disregard this element of our population and reach the highest success. I but convey to you, Mr. President and Directors, the sentiment of the masses of my race when I say that in no way have the value and manhood of the American Negro been more fittingly and generously recognized than by the managers of this magnificent exposition at every stage of its progress. It is a recognition that will do more to cement the friendship of the two races than any occurrence since the dawn of our freedom.

Not only this, but the opportunity here afforded will awaken among us a new era of industrial progress. Ignorant and inexperienced, it is not strange that in the first years of our new life we began at the top instead of at the bottom; that a seat in Congress or the state legislature was more sought than real estate or industrial skill; that the political convention or stump speaking had more attractions than starting a dairy farm or truck garden.

A ship lost at sea for many days suddenly sighted a friendly vessel. From the mast of the unfortunate vessel was seen a signal: "Water, water; we die of thirst!" The answer from the friendly vessel at once came back: "Cast down your bucket where you are." A second time the signal, "Water, water, send us water!" ran up from the distressed vessel, and was answered: "Cast down your bucket where you are." And a third and fourth signal for water was answered: "Cast down your bucket where you are." The captain of the distressed vessel, at last heeding the injunction, cast down his bucket, and it came up full of fresh, sparkling water from the mouth of the Amazon River.

To those of my race who depend on bettering their condition in a foreign land or who underestimate the importance of cultivating friendly relations with the Southern white man, who is their next-door neighbor, I would say: Cast down your bucket where you are. Cast it down in making friends, in every manly way, of the people of all races by whom we are surrounded. Cast it down in agriculture, mechanics, in commerce, in domestic service, and in the professions. And in this connection, it is well to bear in mind that whatever other sins the South may be called to bear, when it comes to business, pure and simple, it is in the South that the Negro is given a man's chance in the commercial world, and in nothing is this exposition more eloquent than in emphasizing this chance.

Our greatest danger is that, in the great leap from slavery to freedom, we may overlook the fact that the masses of us are to live by the productions of our hands and fail to keep in mind that we shall prosper in proportion as we learn to dignify and glorify common labor, and put brains and skill into the common occupations of life; shall prosper in proportion as we learn to draw the line between the superficial and the substantial, the ornamental gewgaws of life and the useful. No race can prosper till it learns that there is as much dignity in tilling a field as in writing a poem. It is at the bottom of life we must begin, and not at the top. Nor should we permit our grievances to overshadow our opportunities.

To those of the white race who look to the incoming of those of foreign birth and strange tongue and habits for the prosperity of the South, were I permitted, I would repeat what I say to my own race, "Cast down your bucket where you are." Cast it down among the 8 million Negroes whose habits you know, whose fidelity and love you have tested in days when to have proved treacherous meant the ruin of your firesides. Cast down your bucket among these people who have, without strikes and labor wars, tilled your fields, cleared your forests, builded your railroads and cities, and brought forth treasures from the bowels of the earth and helped make possible this magnificent representation of the progress of the South. Casting down your bucket among my people, helping and encouraging them as you are doing on these grounds and, with education of head, hand, and heart, you will find that they will buy your surplus land, make blossom the waste places in your fields, and run your factories.

While doing this, you can be sure in the future, as in the past, that you and your families will be surrounded by the most patient, faithful, law-abiding, and unresentful people that the world has seen, As we have proved our loyalty to you in the past, in nursing your children, watching by the sickbed of your mothers and fathers, and often following them with tear-dimmed eyes to their graves, so in the future, in our humble way, we shall stand by you with a devotion that no foreigner can approach, ready to lay down our lives, if need be, in defense of yours; interlacing our industrial, commercial, civil, and religious life with yours in a way that shall make the interests of both races one. In all things that are purely social we can be as separate as the fingers, yet one as the hand in all things essential to mutual progress.

There is no defense or security for any of us except in the highest intelligence and development of all. If anywhere there are efforts tending to curtail the fullest growth of the Negro, let these efforts be turned into stimulating, encouraging, and making him the most useful and intelligent citizen. Effort or means so invested will pay a thousand percent interest. These efforts will be twice blessed—"blessing him that gives and him that takes." . . .

Nearly 16 millions of hands will aid you in pulling the load upward, or they will pull against you the load downward. We shall constitute one-third and more of the ignorance and crime of the South, or one-third its intelligence and progress; we shall contribute one-third to the business and industrial prosperity of the South, or we shall prove a veritable body of death, stagnating, depressing, retarding every effort to advance the body politic.

Gentlemen of the exposition, as we present to you our humble effort at an exhibition of our progress, you must not expect overmuch. Starting thirty years ago with ownership here and there in a few quilts and pumpkins and chickens (gathered from miscellaneous sources), remember: the path that has led from these to the invention and production of agricultural implements, buggies, steam engines, newspapers, books, statuary, carving, paintings, the management of drugstores and banks, has not been trodden without contact with thorns and thistles. While we take pride in what we exhibit as a result of our independent efforts, we do not for a moment forget that our part in this exhibition would fall far short of your expectations but for the constant help that has come to our educational life, not only from the Southern states but especially from Northern philanthropists who have made their gifts a constant stream of blessing and encouragement.

The wisest among my race understand that the agitation of questions of social equality is the extremest folly, and that progress in the enjoyment of all the privileges that will come to us must be the result of severe and constant struggle rather than of artificial forcing. No race that has anything to contribute to the markets of the world is long in any degree ostracized. It is important and right that all privileges of the law be ours, but it is vastly more important that we be prepared for the exercise of these privileges. The opportunity to earn a dollar in a factory just now is worth infinitely more than the opportunity to spend a dollar in an opera house.

In conclusion, may I repeat that nothing in thirty years has given us more hope and encouragement and drawn us so near to you of the white race as this opportunity offered by the exposition; and here bending, as it were, over the altar that represents the results of the struggles of your race and mine, both starting practically empty-handed three decades ago, I pledge that, in your effort to work out the great and intricate problem which God has laid at the doors of the South, you shall have at all times the patient, sympathetic help of my race. Only let this be constantly in mind that, while from representations in these buildings of the product of field, of forest, of mine, of factory, letters, and art, much good will come—yet far above and beyond material benefits will be that higher good, that let us pray God will come, in a blotting out of sectional differences and racial animosities and suspicions, in a determination to administer absolute justice, in a willing obedience among all classes to the mandates of law. This, coupled with our material prosperity, will bring into our beloved South a new heaven and a new earth.

IDA B. WELLS-BARNETT

"THIS AWFUL SLAUGHTER"

Between 1885 and 1894, seventeen hundred African Americans were lynched. This willful taking of human life aroused Ida B. Wells-Barnett (1862–1931) to become a heroic fighter against such outrageous injustice to her people. In conducting her one-woman crusade, she became one of Booker T. Washington's most militant opponents.

Wells was no more than nineteen years of age when, as editor of the *Memphis Free Speech*, she began her campaign. Eventually she became half-owner of the paper. Though threatened by white supremacists, she reported lynchings whenever they occurred. In one report, she charged that the lynching of three successful black grocers was the work of their white competitors.

She was driven out of town by angry whites and her newspaper shop destroyed. Settling in Chicago, Wells joined the *Chicago Conservator*, where she resumed publishing her reports. Meanwhile, she began lecturing throughout the northern part of the country and in Europe about the crime of lynching.

Ida B. Wells-Barnett was an active member of the Niagara Movement, which challenged Booker T. Washington's philosophy. She helped found the National Association for the Advancement of Colored People and delivered the following address at the NAACP's first annual conference, which began May 9, 1909, in Atlanta, Georgia.

THE LYNCHING RECORD for a quarter of a century merits the thoughtful study of the American people. It presents three salient facts:

First, lynching is color-line murder. Second, crimes against women is the excuse, not the cause. Third, it is a national crime and requires a national remedy.

Proof that lynching follows the color line is to be found in the statistics which have been kept for the past twenty-five years. During the few years preceding this period and while frontier lynch law existed, the executions showed a majority of white victims. Later, however, as law courts and authorized judiciary extended into the far West, lynch law rapidly abated, and its white victims became few and far between.

Just as the lynch-law regime came to a close in the West, a new mob movement started in the South. This was wholly political, its purpose being to suppress the colored vote by intimidation and murder. Thousands of assassins banded together under the name of Ku Klux Klans, "Midnight Raiders," "Knights of the Golden Circle," et cetera, et cetera, spread a reign of terror, by beating, shooting and killing colored people by the thousands. In a few years, the purpose was accomplished, and the black vote was suppressed. But mob murder continued.

From 1882, in which year fifty-two were lynched, down to the present, lynching has been along the color line. Mob murder increased yearly until in 1892 more than two hundred victims were lynched and statistics show that 3,284 men, women and children have been put to death in this quarter of a century. During the last ten years from 1899 to 1908 inclusive the number lynched was 959. Of this number 102 were white, while the colored victims numbered 857. No other nation, civilized or savage, burns its criminals; only under the Stars and Stripes is the human holocaust possible. Twenty-eight human beings burned at the stake, one of them a woman and two of them children, is the awful indictment against American civilization—the gruesome tribute which the nation pays to the color line.

Why is mob murder permitted by a Christian nation? What is the cause of this awful slaughter? This question is answered almost daily—always the same shameless falsehood that "Negroes are lynched to protect womanhood." Standing before a Chautauqua assemblage, John Temple Graves, at once champion of lynching and apologist for lynchers, said: "The mob stands today as the most potential bulwark between the women of the South and such a carnival of crime as would infuriate the world and precipitate the annihilation of the Negro race." This is the never-varying answer of lynchers and their apologists. All know that it is untrue. The cowardly lyncher revels in murder, then seeks to shield himself from public execration by claiming devotion to woman. But truth is mighty and the lynching record discloses the hypocrisy of the lyncher as well as his crime.

The Springfield, Illinois, mob rioted for two days, the militia of the entire state was called out, two men were lynched, hundreds of people driven from their homes, all because a white woman said a Negro assaulted her. A mad mob went to the jail, tried to lynch the victim of her charge and, not being able to find him, proceeded to pillage and burn the town and to lynch two innocent men. Later, after the police had found that the woman's charge was false, she published a retraction, the indictment was dismissed and the intended victim discharged. But the lynched victims were dead. Hundreds were homeless and Illinois was disgraced.

As a final and complete refutation of the charge that lynching is occasioned by crimes against women, a partial record of lynchings is cited; 285 persons were lynched for causes as follows:

Unknown cause, 92; no cause, 10; race prejudice, 49 miscegenation, 7; informing, 12; making threats, 11; keeping saloon, 3; practicing fraud, 5; practicing voodooism, 2; bad reputation, 8; unpopularity, 3; mistaken identity, 5; using improper language, 3; violation of contract, 1; writing insulting letter, 2; eloping, 2; poisoning horse, 1; poisoning well, 2; by white caps, 9; vigilantes, 14; Indians, 1; moonshining, 1; refusing evidence, 2; political causes, 5; disputing, 1 disobeying quarantine regulations, 2; slapping a child, 1; turning state's evidence, 3; protecting a Negro, 1; to prevent giving evidence, 1; knowledge of larceny, 1; writing letter to white woman, 1; asking white woman to marry, 1; jilting girl, 1; having smallpox, 1; concealing criminal, 2; threatening political exposure, 1; self-defense, 6; cruelty, 1; insulting language to woman, 5; quarreling with white man, 2; colonizing Negroes, 1; throwing stones, 1; quarreling, 1; gambling, 1.

Is there a remedy, or will the nation confess that it cannot protect its protectors at home as well as abroad? Various remedies have been suggested to abolish the lynching infamy, but year after year, the butchery of men, women and children continues in spite of plea and protest. Education is suggested as a preventive, but it is as grave a crime to murder an ignorant man as it is a scholar. True, few educated men have been lynched, but the hue and cry once started stops at no bounds, as was clearly shown by the lynchings in Atlanta, and in Springfield, Illinois.

Agitation, though helpful, will not alone stop the crime. Year after year statistics are published, meetings are held, resolutions are adopted and yet lynchings go on. Public sentiment does measurably decrease the sway of mob law, but the irresponsible bloodthirsty criminals who swept through the streets of Springfield, beating an inoffensive law-abiding citizen to death in one part of the town, and in another torturing and shooting to death a man who for threescore years had made a reputation for honesty, integrity and sobriety, had raised a family and had accumulated property, were not deterred from their heinous crimes by either education or agitation.

The only certain remedy is an appeal to law. Lawbreakers must be made to know that human life is sacred and that every citizen of this country is first a citizen of the United States and secondly a citizen of the state in which he belongs. This nation must assert itself and defend its federal citizenship at home as well as abroad. The strong arm of the government must reach across state lines whenever unbridled lawlessness defies state laws and must give to the individual citizen under the Stars and Stripes the same measure of protection which it gives to him when he travels in foreign lands.

Federal protection of American citizenship is the remedy for lynching. Foreigners are rarely lynched in America. If, by mistake, one is lynched, the national government quickly pays the damages. The recent agitation in California against the Japanese compelled this nation to recognize that federal power must yet assert itself to protect the nation from the treason of sovereign states. Thousands of American citizens have been put to death and no President has yet raised his hand in effective protest, but a simple insult to a native of Japan was quite sufficient to stir the government at Washington to prevent the threatened wrong. If the government has power to protect a foreigner from insult, certainly it has power to save a citizen's life.

The practical remedy has been more than once suggested in Congress. Senator Gallinger, of New Hampshire, in a resolution introduced in Congress called for an investigation "with the view of ascertaining whether there is a remedy for lynching which Congress may apply." The Senate Committee has under consideration a bill drawn by A. E. Pillsbury, formerly Attorney General of Massachusetts, providing for federal prosecution of lynchers in cases where the state fails to protect citizens or foreigners. Both of these resolutions indicate that the attention of the nation has been called to this phase of the lynching question.

As a final word, it would be a beginning in the right direction if this conference can see its way clear to establish a bureau for the investigation and publication of the details of every lynching, so that the public could know that an influential body of citizens has made it a duty to give the widest publicity to the facts in each case; that it will make an effort to secure expressions of opinion all over the country against lynching for the sake of the country's fair name; and lastly, but by no means least, to try to influence the daily papers of the country to refuse to become accessory to mobs either before or after the fact.

Several of the greatest riots and most brutal burnt offerings of the mobs have been suggested and incited by the daily papers of the offending community. If the newspaper which suggests lynching in its accounts of an alleged crime, could be held legally as well as morally responsible for reporting that "threats of lynching were heard"; or, "it is feared that if the guilty one is caught, he will be lynched"; or, "there were cries of 'lynch him,' and the only reason the threat was not carried out was because no leader appeared," a long step toward a remedy will have been taken.

In a multitude of counsel there is wisdom. Upon the grave question presented by the slaughter of innocent men, women and children there should be an honest, courageous conference of patriotic, law-abiding citizens anxious to punish crime promptly, impartially and by due process of law, also to make life, liberty and property secure against mob rule.

Time was when lynching appeared to be sectional, but now it is national—a blight upon our nation, mocking our laws and disgracing our Christianity. "With malice toward none but with charity for all" let us undertake the work of making the "law of the land" effective and supreme upon every foot of American soil—a shield to the innocent; and to the guilty, punishment swift and sure.

MARCUS GARVEY

"THE PRINCIPLES OF THE UNIVERSAL NEGRO IMPROVEMENT ASSOCIATION"

A self-educated, self-proclaimed black leader, Marcus Garvey (1887–1940) was born and raised in Jamaica. In 1911, he founded his Universal Negro Improvement Association, whose purpose was to "bring Negroes together for the building up of a nation of their own."[10] In 1916, Garvey moved to Harlem, in New York City, where he started a "back-to-Africa" movement that grew into a crusade. He then bought the Black Star line of steamships, which were "owned, controlled and manned by Negroes to reach Negro people of the world."[11]

Eventually Garvey faced criminal charges relating to his shipping company and spent time in prison before being deported. By the time of his conviction, however, an estimated one to four million African Americans had become part of his movement.

In a speech delivered in New York City on November 25, 1922, Garvey explained the reasons and purpose of the Universal Negro Improvement Association. Part of that speech follows.

THE UNIVERSAL NEGRO IMPROVEMENT ASSOCIATION stands for the *bigger brotherhood*; the Universal Negro Improvement Association stands for human rights, not only for Negroes, but for all races. The Universal Negro Improvement Association believes in the rights of not only the black race, but the white race, the yellow race and the brown race. The Universal Negro Improvement Association believes that the white man has as much right to be considered, the yellow man has as much right to be considered, the brown man has as much right to be considered as well as the black man of Africa. In view of the fact that the black man of Africa has contributed as much to the world as the white man of Europe and the brown man and yellow man of Asia, we of the Universal Negro Improvement Association demand that the white, yellow and brown races give to the black man his place in the civilization of the world. We ask for nothing more than the rights of four hundred million Negroes. We are not seeking, as I said before, to destroy or disrupt the society or the government of other races, but we are determined that four hundred million of us shall unite ourselves to free our motherland from the grasp of the invader. We of the Universal Negro Improvement Association are determined to unite four hundred million Negroes for their own industrial, political, social and religious emancipation.

We of the Universal Negro Improvement Association are determined to unite the four hundred million Negroes of the world to give expression to their own feeling; we are determined to unite the four hundred million Negroes of the world for the purpose of building a civilization of their own. And in that effort we desire to bring together the fifteen million of the United States, the one hundred and eighty million in Asia, the West Indies and Central and South America, and the two hundred million in Africa. We are looking toward political freedom on the continent of Africa, the land of our fathers. . . .

The Universal Negro Improvement Association is not

seeking to build up another government within the bounds or borders of the United States of America. The Universal Negro Improvement Association is not seeking to disrupt any organized system of government, but the Association is determined to bring Negroes together for the building-up of a nation of their own. And why? Because we have been forced to it. We have been forced to it throughout the world; not only in America, not only in Europe, not only in the British Empire, but wheresoever the black man happens to find himself, he has been forced to do for himself.

To talk about government is a little more than some of our people can appreciate just at this time. The average man does not think that way, just because he finds himself a citizen or a subject of some country. He seems to say, "Why should there be need for any other government?" We are French, English or American. But we of the U.N.I.A. have studied seriously this question of nationality among Negroes—this American nationality, this British nationality, this French, Italian or Spanish nationality—and have discovered that it counts for nought when that nationality comes in conflict with the racial idealism of the group that rules. When our interests clash with those of the ruling faction, then we find that we have absolutely no rights. In times of peace, when everything is all right, Negroes have a hard time, wherever we go, wheresoever we find ourselves, getting those rights that belong to us, in common with others whom we claim as fellow citizens; getting that consideration that should be ours by right of the constitution, by right of the law; but in the time of trouble they make us all partners in the cause, as happened in the last war, when we were partners, whether British, French or American Negroes. And we were told that we must forget everything in an effort to save the nation.

We have saved many nations in this manner, and we have lost our lives doing that before. Hundreds of

A modern traditional West African musician-storyteller,
or *griot*, with his *kora*, a harplike instrument made from a
dried gourd and cowhide. Without the griot there might have
been no jazz singer, blues musician, gospel star, rock 'n' roll
band, rap singer—or, perhaps, great black orators.

Black preachers preaching to slaves were a common sight on southern plantations before emancipation. The tradition of the fiery black minister has continued through such contemporary African-American leaders as Martin Luther King, Jr., Malcolm X, and Jesse Jackson, all ministers.

At the Colored National Conventions, African Americans used their speech-making abilities to denounce slavery.

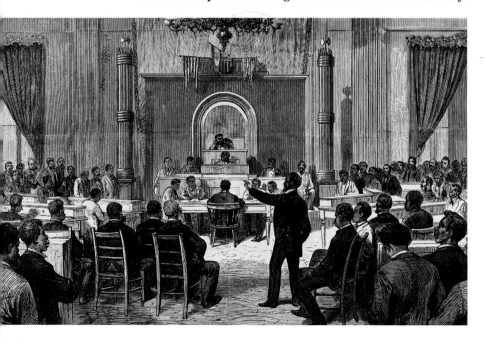

The National Association for the Advancement of
Colored People grew out of the Niagara Movement,
some of whose participants are pictured here in front of
Niagara Falls. In the second row, second from the right,
is W.E.B. Du Bois, one of the great African-American
leaders, writers, and orators of the twentieth century.

Juſt imported from Africa, by Capt. RICHARDS and now on board his Sloop at Coenties's-Dock, a parcel of very fine young healthy

SLAVES,

To be ſold by HENRY C. BOGART, next Door to Mr. John Vanderſpiegle.----He has alſo Molaſſes for Sale.

Slavery was the greatest motivating force behind the development of black orators. Here, a handbill announces the forthcoming sale of newly arrived slaves from Africa.

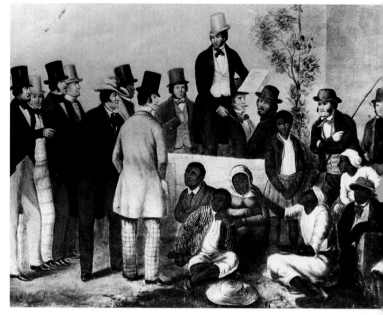

A slave auction

Below: Slaves working sweet potato fields on a South Carolina plantation in 1862.

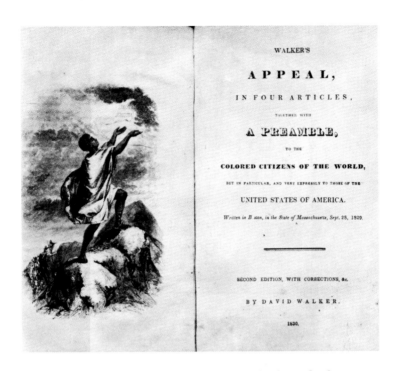

Walker's Appeal, published in 1829, dealt with slavery.
It was one of the first examples demonstrating
the power of black oratory—put into writing.

The Reverend Peter Williams, Jr.,
standing in the doorway of the
church, argued that blacks were
Americans and opposed
sending them back to Africa.

After passage of the Fugitive Slave Law of 1850, the Reverend Jermain Wesley Loguen announced publicly: "I am a fugitive slave from Tennessee. My master is Manasseth Loguen."

John Sweat Rock, a Boston physician and attorney

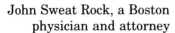

Sojourner Truth, the outspoken abolitionist and feminist, shown with President Abraham Lincoln

Robert B. Elliott served in the
House of Representatives
during Reconstruction.

Blanche Kelso Bruce,
elected senator from
Mississippi in 1874

Frederick Douglass was one
of the most famous black
leaders and orators of
the nineteenth century.

Mary Church Terrell, the first
president of the National
Association of Colored Women

After the Civil War, a major horror for the
newly liberated African Americans was
lynching and other forms of mob violence . . .

. . . while overt segregation
was the prime obstacle
to equality.

Booker T. Washington (1856–1915), the most famous black leader of his generation, believed that African Americans had to better themselves and not challenge the white establishment.

Ida B. Wells-Barnett, one of the most militant fighters against lynching

Marcus Garvey, founder of the Universal Negro Improvement Association, started a back-to-Africa movement in the early part of the twentieth century. He was a large man and a man of many words.

W.E.B. Du Bois, one of the founders of the NAACP and one of the architects of the fight for black equality in the twentieth century, believed, contrary to Booker T. Washington, that blacks had to boldly fight for their rights as American citizens.

The 1960s ushered in a movement for civil rights, as African
Americans throughout the country—both south (top) and
north—demonstrated for equality, respect, and opportunity.

Martin Luther King, Jr., one of the great orators of all time, represented the culmination of the tradition of the fiery African-American preacher/leader/orator. He used his abilities to apply the nonviolent ideas and practices of Mahatma Gandhi to the struggle for equality in America. In doing so he helped launch the civil rights revolution.

Stokely Carmichael, now known as Kwame Toure, a former leader of the Student Nonviolent Coordinating Committee and the originator of the concept of black power, has been a dynamic speaker since the 1960s.

During his lifetime, the expatriate writer James Baldwin was one of the most perceptive, articulate, and outspoken critics of racism in America.

"Fighting" Shirley Chisholm, the first black woman to serve in Congress, shown with President Lyndon B. Johnson in 1969.

Malcolm X, the powerful and militant leader, was such a threat to both blacks and whites alike that he was assassinated.

James Forman led the Student Nonviolent Coordinating Committee in the 1960s at the height of its power, when it was organizing whites and blacks to go south to fight for black civil rights.

In 1979, marchers observed the twenty-fifth anniversary of the Supreme Court decision outlawing school segregation.

The fight was and still is not over yet: Although African Americans have come a long way, from electing Harold Washington the first black mayor of Chicago in 1983 . . .

. . . to becoming an astronaut . . .

. . . millions are discriminated against, live below
the poverty line, and live in abject neighborhoods.

Vernon F. Jordan, Jr., former executive director of the National Urban League, a black organization devoted to improving the lives of African Americans

Barbara Jordan, the first African American elected to the Texas state senate, also served as its president pro tempore. She went on to serve in the U.S. House of Representatives and built a reputation as one of the most dynamic and articulate political leaders in the United States.

Angela Y. Davis, a controversial political activist in the 1970s, continues to be a militant supporter of racial equality, workers' rights, and similar causes.

The Reverend Jesse Jackson
worked with Dr. Martin
Luther King, Jr., in the 1960s,
and twice ran for the presidency
of the United States. He is an
outstanding organizer, leader,
and orator.

thousands—nay, millions of black men, lie buried under the ground due to that old-time camouflage of saving the nation. We saved the British Empire; we saved the French Empire; we saved this glorious country more than once; and all that we have received for our sacrifices, all that we have received for what we have done even in giving up our lives, is just what you are receiving now, just what I am receiving now.

You and I fare no better in America, in the British Empire, or in any other part of the white world; we fare no better than any black man wheresoever he shows his head. And why? Because we have been satisfied to allow ourselves to be led, educated, to be directed by the other fellow, who has always sought to lead in the world in that direction that would satisfy him and strengthen his position. We have allowed ourselves for the last five hundred years to be a race of followers, following every race that has led in the direction that would make them more secure.

The U.N.I.A. is reversing the old-time order of things. We refuse to be followers any more. We are leading ourselves. That means, if any saving is to be done, later on, whether it is saving this one nation or that one government, we are going to seek a method of saving Africa first. Why? And why Africa? Because Africa has become the grand prize of the nations. Africa has become the big game of the nation hunters. Today Africa looms as the greatest commercial, industrial and political prize in the world. . . .

W.E.B. DU BOIS

"IN THE PEOPLE WE HAVE THE REAL SOURCE OF ... ENDLESS LIFE AND UNBOUNDED WISDOM"

A brilliant historian, critic, editor, and essayist, W.E.B. Du Bois (1868–1963) was also a militant African-American leader. Throughout his life, he exercised a deep interest in the social affairs of his people. He helped found the National Association for the Advancement of Colored People (NAACP), the oldest civil rights organization in the United States.

One of the many rights for which Du Bois fought was the right of every American to vote, a right denied African Americans in the South. Women were also denied this right by a law of the land. Du Bois at the turn of the twentieth century recognized both African Americans and women as victims of prejudice. The address he gave at the Convention of the National Women's Suffrage Association in New York City in 1912 compared the disenfranchisement of African Americans in the South with that of women throughout the nation.

THE MERE FACT that democratic government has spread in the past and is still spreading does not prove that those concerned in its spread always realize the broader foundations of the argument that supports it. Usually nations are dealing with concrete groups whose enfranchisement is advocated and the arguments against the step fall under these categories:

    a. The persons in the group are too ignorant to vote intelligently.

    b. The persons are too inexperienced to be trusted with so great responsibility.

    c. The persons would misuse the privilege.

    d. They do not need the ballot.

    e. They do not want the right to vote.

The obvious assumptions behind these objections are that only the intelligent should have the right to vote; that voters should possess some technical knowledge of the government; that only those should have the franchise who do not misuse it for selfish or other ends, and who need the ballot for their good and are anxious to have it.

No sooner, however, do we express these qualifications than it is manifest that these are not such qualifications as one could reasonably require. They are in reality arguments addressed to the self-interest of the present rulers and calculated to show that sharing their prerogative with another group will not disturb or prejudice their present power and perquisites.

While it is manifestly the part of practical political wisdom thus to cajole the present ruler, the weapon used is dangerous and the argument is only partially valid. The real underlying and eternally valid arguments for extending as far as possible the participation of human beings in their own government must lie deeper than these phrases and be more carefully framed. If this is done then the advance of democracy will be made easier and more effective since we can scrutinize the essential facts and not be distracted by immaterial suggestions.

What is then the essential argument for extending

the right to vote? We may possibly reach it by clearing away the misapprehensions that lurk in the arguments mentioned above.

For instance, we say easily, "The ignorant ought not to vote." We mean to say, "There should be in the state, no grown person of sound mind who is not intelligent enough to vote." These two statements may seem to be essentially the same, but they have vastly different implications. In the one case we cast the ignorant aside. They ought not to vote and the implication is that it is their fault. Their interests, we assume will be looked after by others and if they are not, we acknowledge no responsibility. On the other hand, if we stress the responsibility of the state for the education of its citizens as prior to political rights, then the conclusion is that if a state allows its citizens to grow up in ignorance it ought to suffer from an ignorant ballot: that it is the threat of ignorant voters that makes good schools.

The second argument that experience is a necessary prerequisite to voting is absurd. According to this we should have no new voters, unless we assume that the capacity to rule is hereditary. Such assumptions have been made in the past with regard to certain races and one sex. It can scarcely be said, however, that any adequate proof exists which proves that only Englishmen or only persons of the male sex are capable of learning to take part in democratic government. When we consider that the civilized world today is being ruled by classes who were pronounced utterly incapable of self-rule or of being trained for self-rule a century ago, we must conclude that the ability to rule is, on the whole, a matter of individual social training and that consequently there must always be a part of the body politic without experience who must be trained by the others. In voting as in other matters we learn by doing. It is to be expected that every new voting class and every new democracy will make its costly and ridiculous mistakes—will pass through demagoguery, extravagance, "boss" rule, bribery and the like; but it is through such experience that voters learn to rule and the cost although vast is not excessive if the end is finally gained.

Thus we see that ignorance is a warning and a public responsibility rather than a permanent excuse for disfranchisement, save in the case of the small number who cannot be educated; that inexperience can only be cured by experience and is consequently no reason for disfranchisement; and that misuse of the ballot is perhaps the most effective way of teaching its right use.

There are, however, people who insist on regarding the franchise not as a necessity for the many but as the privilege of the few. They say of persons and classes, "They do not need the ballot." This is often said of women. It is argued that everything that women might do for themselves with the ballot can be done for them; that they have influence and friends "at court," and that their enfranchisement would simply double the number of ballots. So, too, we are told that Negroes can have done for them by others all that they could possibly do for themselves with the ballot, and much more because the whites are more intelligent.

Further than this it is argued that many of the disfranchised recognize this. "Women do not want the ballot," has been a very effective counter war cry; so much so that many a man has taken refuge in the declaration, "When they want to vote, why then—."

Such phrases show so curious a misapprehension of the foundations of the argument for democracy that this argument must be continually restated and emphasized. We must remember that if the theory of democracy is correct, the right to vote is not merely a privilege, not simply a method of meeting the needs of a particular group, and least of all a matter of recognized want or desire. Democracy is a method of realizing the broadest measure of justice to all human beings. The world has in the past attempted various methods of attaining this end, most of which can be summed up in three categories:

The method of the benevolent tyrant
"　　"　　"　" select few
"　　"　　"　" excluded groups.

The method of entrusting the government of a people to a strong ruler has great advantages when the ruler combines strength with ability, unselfish devotion to the public good and knowledge of what that good calls for. Such a combination is, however, rare and the selection of the right ruler is very difficult. To leave the selection to force is to put a premium on physical strength, chance and intrigue; to make the selection a matter of birth simply transfers the real power from sovereign to selected minister. Inevitably the choice of real rulers must fall on electors.

Then comes the problem. Who shall elect? The earlier answer was: a select few, such as the wise, the best born, the able. Many people assume that it was corruption that made such aristocracies fail. By no means. The best and most effective aristocracy, like the best monarchy, suffered from lack of knowledge; they did not know or understand the needs of the people, and they could not find out, for in the last analysis only the man himself, however humble, knows his own condition. He may not know how to remedy it, he may not realize just what is the matter, but he knows when something hurts, and he alone knows how that hurt feels. Or if, sunk below feeling or comprehension or complaint, he does not even know that he is hurt, God help his country, for it not only lacks knowledge, but has destroyed some of the sources of knowledge!

So soon as a nation discovers that it holds in the heads and hearts of its individual citizens the vast mine of knowledge out of which it may build a just government, then more and more it calls those citizens to select their rulers and judge the justice of their acts.

Even here, however, the temptation is to ask only

for the wisdom of citizens of a certain grade, or those of recognized worth. Continually some classes are tacitly or expressly excluded. Thus women have been regularly excluded from modern democracy, because of custom, because of the persistent theory of female subjection, and because it was argued that their husbands or other male folk would look to their interests. Now manifestly most husbands, fathers and brothers will so far as they know how, or so far as they realize women's needs look after them. But remember that the foundation of the argument is that in the last analysis only the sufferer knows his sufferings, and that no state can be strong which excludes from its expressed wisdom, the knowledge possessed by mothers, wives and daughters. Certainly we have but to view the unsatisfactory relations of the sexes the world over and the problem of children, to realize how desperately we need this excluded wisdom.

The same argument applies to other excluded groups: if a race like the Negro race is excluded from the ballot, then so far as that race is a part of the economic and social organization of the land, the feeling and the experience of that race is absolutely necessary to the realization of the broadest justice for all citizens. Or if the "submerged tenth" be excluded, then again there is lost experience of untold value, and the submerged must be raised rapidly to a plane where they can speak for themselves.

In the same way and for the same reason children must be educated, insanity prevented and only those put under guardianship of others who can in no way be trained to speak for themselves.

The real argument for democracy is then that in the people we have the real source of that endless life and unbounded wisdom which the real ruler of men must have. A given people today may not be intelligent, but through a democratic government that recognizes not only the worth of the individual to himself but the worth of his feelings and experiences to all, they can educate not only the individual unit, but generation after generation until they accumulate vast stores of wisdom. Democracy alone is the method of storing the whole experience of the race for the benefit of the future, and if democracy tries to exclude women or Negroes or the poor or any class because of innate characteristics which do not interfere with intelligence then that democracy cripples itself and belies its name.

From this point of view we can easily see the weakness and strength of current criticism of extensions of the ballot. It is the business of a modern government to see to it, *first*, that the number of the ignorant within its bounds is reduced to the very smallest number. *Secondly*, it is the duty of every such government to extend as quickly as possible the number of grown persons of mature age who can vote. Such possible voters must be regarded not as sharers of a limited treasure, but as sources of new national wisdom and strength.

The addition of the new wisdom, the new points of view and new interests must of course be, from time to time, bewildering and confusing. Today those who have a voice in the body politic have expressed their wishes and sufferings. The result has been a more or less effective balancing of their conflicting interests. The appearance of new interests and complaints means disarrangement and confusion to the older equilibrium. But this is not in itself evil—it is the inevitable preliminary step to that larger equilibrium in which the interests of no human soul will be neglected. These interests will not, surely, be all fully realized but they will be recognized and given as full weight as the conflicting interests of others will allow. The problem of government thereafter will be to reduce the necessary conflict of human interests to the minimum.

From such a point of view one easily sees the strength of the demand for the ballot on the part of certain disfranchised classes. When women ask for the ballot they are asking not a privilege but a necessity. You may not see the necessity; you may easily argue that women do not need to vote. Indeed the women themselves in considerable number may feel the same. Nevertheless they do need the ballot. They need it to right the balance of a world sadly awry because of its brutal neglect of the rights of women and children. With the best will and knowledge no man can know women's wants as well as women themselves. To disfranchise them is deliberately to turn from knowledge and grope in ignorance.

So too with American Negroes: the South continually insists that a benevolent guardianship of whites over blacks is the ideal thing. They assume that white people not only know better what Negroes need than Negroes themselves, but are anxious to supply those needs. As a result, instead of knowledge they grope in ignorance and helplessness. They cannot "understand" the Negro, they cannot protect him from cheating and lynching and in general instead of loving guardianship, we see anarchy and exploitation. If the Negro could speak for himself in the South instead of being spoken for: if he could defend himself instead of having to depend on the chance sympathy of white citizens, how much healthier growth of democracy the South would have.

It is not for a moment to be assumed that enfranchising women would not cost something. It would for many years confuse our politics. It would change the composition of family and social life. It would admit to the ballot thousands of inexperienced persons unable to vote intelligently. Above all it would interfere with some of the present prerogatives of men and probably for some time to come annoy them considerably.

So, too, Negro enfranchisement meant Reconstruction with its theft, bribery and incompetency. It would mean today that black men in the South would have to be treated with consideration, have their wishes more respected and their manhood recognized. Every white southerner who wants peons beneath him, who believes in hereditary menials and a privileged aristocracy, or who hates certain races because of their characteristics, would resent this.

Notwithstanding this, if America is ever to become a government built on the broadest justice to every citizen, then every citizen must be enfranchised. There may be temporary exclusions until the ignorant or their children are taught, or to avoid too sudden an influx of inexperienced voters. But such exclusions can be but temporary if justice is to prevail.

While many of those seeking enfranchisement recognize the broad demand of justice for all human beings which underlies their argument, they are often tempted by the exigencies of the situation to ignore the application of those underlying principles to any but themselves, or even to deny and attack the justice of equally just demands for the ballot. The advocates of woman suffrage have continually been in great danger of asking the ballot not because they are citizens, but because they occupy a certain social position, are of a certain grade of intelligence, or are "white." Continually it has been said in America, "If paupers and Negroes vote why not college-bred women of wealth and position?" The assumption is that such a woman has superior right to have her interests represented in the nation and that Negroes and paupers have few rights which society leaders are bound to respect. So, too, many colored people, in arguing their own enfranchisement, are willing to be counted against the enfranchisement of women or foreigners or the unfortunate. Such argument or neglect is both false and dangerous, and while its phrasing may be effective at times it represents a climbing of one class on the misery of another.

The insistent call of democracy is ringing in the ears of all people today as never before in spite of the hard experiences of the past. The cure for the ills of democracy is seen to be more democracy. We are rapidly changing from a form of social control dictated by the interests of a few to one dictated by the interests of a large and larger majority. Not only is this true in what is usually called politics but also in industry. In fact our political interests are becoming more and more industrial and our industry is assuming larger and larger political aspects. In the industrial world we are still under the rule of the strong monarch, with at most the mitigation of the power of the selected few. We feel the consequent confusion. We lack knowledge of industrial conditions. We have no standard of industrial justice. Whence shall knowledge and standards come? Through democracy. Through having the rights and wishes of every worker represented in the power that controls industry. This will be hard to attain. The passing of the strong monarchs in industry as in politics will spell anarchy in many places, but social justice will eventually come. How necessary then to build a state of the broadest democracy to cope with the industrial problem within nations and between nations and races.

THE CIVIL RIGHTS REVOLUTION

There was a lesson to be learned from American history, one that did not escape African Americans. It was the effectiveness of civil disobedience in eliminating civil wrongs.

African Americans had experienced American's wars as witnesses and participants, though they shared in comparatively few of the economic benefits of these wars. But by forcing the hand of those practicing racial bigotry, African Americans had gained the power of the vote. In this way, they served notice that black Americans were citizens entitled to all the rights and privileges of white Americans. Though proud of what they had achieved, African Americans could hardly feel satisfied.

Martin Luther King, Jr., voiced this dissatisfaction in a historic address at the foot of the Lincoln Memorial in Washington, D.C. It was an inspired speech at a time of growing pride and expectation. But it was also a time when old, established civil rights organizations, such as the National Association for the Advancement of Colored

People and the Urban League, and more militant groups, such as the Student Nonviolent Coordinating Committee (SNCC), the Congress of Racial Equality (CORE), and the Black Muslims, were in conflict.

Beginning in the 1960s, more-aggressive leaders emerged. Some, like James Baldwin, were aggressive of mind. Others, such as Malcolm X, called for a separate black society independent from whites. This idea was embraced as "Black Power" by young African Americans who were no longer willing to wait for racial equality. They believed the time had come to demand and demonstrate for equal treatment in all public facilities. The victories gained from demonstrations in the South were only the beginning. It was time for African-American leaders to show the way by establishing a revolutionary force of Black Power. Other blacks were more moderate, preferring to work for change within the system—with elected officials and industrial leaders.

JAMES BALDWIN

"A TALK TO TEACHERS"

James Baldwin (1924–1987) was an outstanding writer of novels and plays, in which he dramatized the racial prejudice experienced by African Americans. Perhaps his most effective writing, however, was in essay form, where he took white Americans to task for creating the lie of racism and distorting the history of black-white relations in America.

Although he was not as well known as a speaker, Baldwin was equally effective in this medium. His "A Talk to Teachers," given in 1963 and printed below, was one of his many "messages" to white Americans, who he felt bore the burden of racial guilt. On this occasion, he was returning to his roots to address an audience of teachers in Harlem at a school in the very neighborhood he had lived in as a boy. Sharing the terrible feeling a black child experiences growing up in a New York City ghetto, he points the finger of blame and responsibility at his audience.

LET'S BEGIN BY saying that we are living through a very dangerous time. Everyone in this room is in one way or another aware of that. We are in a revolutionary situation, no matter how unpopular that word has become in this country. The society in which we live is desperately menaced, not by Khrushchev, but from within. So any citizen of this country who figures himself as responsible—and particularly those of you who deal with the minds and hearts of young people—must be prepared to "go for broke." Or to put it another way, you must understand that in the attempt to correct so many generations of bad faith and cruelty, when it is operating not only in the classroom but in society, you will meet the most fantastic, the most brutal, and the most determined resistance. There is no point in pretending that this won't happen.

Since I am talking to schoolteachers and I am not a teacher myself, and in some ways am fairly easily intimidated, I beg you to let me leave that and go back to what I think to be the entire purpose of education in the first place. It would seem to me that when a child is born, if I'm the child's parent, it is my obligation and my high duty to civilize that child. Man is a social animal. He cannot exist without a society. A society, in turn, depends on certain things which everyone within that society takes for granted. Now, the crucial paradox which confronts us here is that the whole process of education occurs within a social framework and is designed to perpetuate the aims of society. Thus, for example, the boys and girls who were born during the era of the Third Reich, when educated to the purposes of the Third Reich, became barbarians. The paradox of education is precisely this—that as one begins to become conscious one begins to examine the society in which he is being educated. The purpose of education, finally, is to create in a person the ability to look at the world for himself, to make his own decisions, to say to himself this is black or this is white, to decide for himself whether there is a God in heaven or not. To ask questions of the universe, and then learn to live with those questions, is the way he achieves his own identity. But no society is really anxious to have that kind of person around. What societies really, ideally, want is a citizenry which will simply obey the rules of society. If a society succeeds in this, that society is about to perish. The obligation of anyone who thinks of himself as responsible is to examine society and try to change it and to fight it—at no matter what risk. This is the only hope society has. This is the only way societies change.

Now, if what I have tried to sketch has any validity, it becomes thoroughly clear, at least to me, that any Negro who is born in this country and undergoes the American educational system runs the risk of becoming schizophrenic. On the one hand he is born in the shadow of the stars and stripes and he is assured it represents a nation which has never lost a war. He pledges allegiance to that flag which guarantees "liberty and justice for all." He is part of a country in which anyone can become president, and so forth. But on the other hand he is also assured by his country and his countrymen that he has never contributed anything to civilization—that his past is nothing more than a record of humiliations gladly endured. He is assumed by the republic that he, his father, his mother, and his ancestors were happy, shiftless, watermelon-eating darkies who loved Mr. Charlie and Miss Ann, that the value he has as a black man is proven by one thing only—his devotion to white people. If you think I am exaggerating, examine the myths which proliferate in this country about Negroes.

All this enters the child's consciousness much sooner than we as adults would like to think it does. As adults, we are easily fooled because we are so anxious to be fooled. But children are very different. Children, not yet aware that it is dangerous to look too deeply at anything, look at everything, look at each other, and draw their own conclusions. They don't have the vocabulary to express what they see, and we, their elders, know how to intimidate them very easily and very soon. But a black child, looking at the world around him, though he cannot know quite what to make of it, is aware that there is a reason why his mother works so hard, why his father is always on edge. He is aware that there is some reason why, if he sits down in the front of the bus, his father or mother slaps him and drags him to the back of the bus. He is aware that there is some terrible weight on his parents' shoulders which menaces him. And it isn't long—in fact it begins when he is in school—before he discovers the shape of his oppression.

Let us say that the child is seven years old and I am his father, and I decide to take him to the zoo, or to Madison Square Garden, or to the U.N. Building, or to any of the tremendous monuments we find all over New York. We get into a bus and we go from where I live on 131st Street and Seventh Avenue downtown through the park and we get into New York City, which is not Harlem. Now, where the boy lives—even if it is a housing project— is in an undesirable neighborhood. If he lives in one of those housing projects of which everyone in New York is so proud, he has at the front door, if not closer, the pimps, the whores, the junkies—in a word, the danger of life in the ghetto. And the child knows this, though he doesn't know why.

I still remember my first sight of New York. It was really another city when I was born—where I was born. We looked down over the Park Avenue streetcar tracks. It was Park Avenue, but I didn't know that Park Avenue meant *downtown*. The Park Avenue I grew up on, which is still standing, is dark and dirty. No one would dream of opening a Tiffany's on that Park Avenue, and when you go downtown you discover that you are literally in the white world. It is rich—or at least it looks rich. It is clean—because they collect garbage downtown. There are doormen. People walk about as though they owned where they are—and indeed they do. And it's a great shock. It's very hard to relate yourself to this. You don't know what it means. You know—you know instinctively—that none of this is for you. You know this before you are told. And who is it for and who is paying for it? And why isn't it for you?

Later on when you become a grocery boy or messenger and you try to enter one of those buildings a man says, "Go to the back door." Still later, if you happen by some odd chance to have a friend in one of those buildings, the man says, "Where's your package?" Now this by no means is the core of the matter. What I'm trying to get at is that by this time the Negro child has had, effectively, almost all the doors of opportunity slammed in his face, and there are very few things he can do about it. He can more or less accept it with an absolutely inarticulate and dangerous rage inside—all the more dangerous because it is never expressed. It is precisely those silent people whom white people see every day of their lives—I mean your porter and your maid, who never say anything more than "Yes, Sir" and "No, Ma'am." They will tell you it's raining if that is what you want to hear, and they will tell you the sun is shining if *that* is what you want to hear. They really hate you—really hate you because in their eyes (and they're right) you stand between them and life. I want to come back to that in a moment. It is the most sinister of the facts, I think, which we now face.

* * *

There is something else the Negro child can do, too. Every street boy—and I was a street boy, so I know—looking at the society which has produced him, looking at the standards of that society which are not honored by anybody, looking at your churches and the government and the politicians, understands that this structure is operated for someone else's benefit—not for his. And there's no reason in it for him. If he is really cunning, really

115

ruthless, really strong—and many of us are—he becomes a kind of criminal. He becomes a kind of criminal because that's the only way he can live. Harlem and every ghetto in this city—every ghetto in this country—is full of people who live outside the law. They wouldn't dream of calling a policeman. They wouldn't, for a moment, listen to any of those professions of which we are so proud on the Fourth of July. They have turned away from this country forever and totally. They live by their wits and really long to see the day when the entire structure comes down.

The point of all this is that black men were brought here as a source of cheap labor. They were indispensable to the economy. In order to justify the fact that men were treated as though they were animals, the white republic had to brainwash itself into believing that they were, indeed, animals and *deserved* to be treated like animals. Therefore it is almost impossible for any Negro child to discover anything about his actual history. The reason is that this "animal," once he suspects his own worth, once he starts believing that he is a man, has begun to attack the entire power structure. This is why America has spent such a long time keeping the Negro in his place. What I am trying to suggest to you is that it was not an accident, it was not an act of God, it was not done by well-meaning people muddling into something which they didn't understand. It was a deliberate policy hammered into place in order to make money from black flesh. And now, in 1963, because we have never faced this fact, we are in intolerable trouble.

The Reconstruction, as I read the evidence, was a bargain between the North and South to this effect: "We've liberated them from the land—and delivered them to the bosses." When we left Mississippi to come North we did not come to freedom. We came to the bottom of the labor market, and we are still there. Even the Depression of the 1930s failed to make a dent in Negroes' relationship to white workers in the labor unions. Even today, so brainwashed is this republic that people seriously ask in what they suppose to be good faith, "What does the Negro want?" I've heard a great many asinine questions in my life, but that is perhaps the most asinine and perhaps the most insulting. But the point here is that people who ask that question, thinking that they ask it in good faith, are really the victims of this conspiracy to make Negroes believe they are less than human.

In order for me to live, I decided very early that some mistake had been made somewhere. I was not a "nigger" even though you called me one. But if I was a "nigger" in your eyes, there was something about *you*—there was something *you* needed. I had to realize when I was very young that I was none of those things I was told I was. I was not, for example, happy. I never touched a watermelon for all kinds of reasons that had been invented by white people, and I knew enough about life by this time to understand that whatever you invent, whatever you project, is you! So where we are now is that a whole country of people believe I'm a "nigger," and I *don't*, and the battle's on! Because if I am not what I've been told I am, then it means that *you're* not what you thought *you* were *either*! And that is the crisis.

It is not really a "Negro revolution" that is upsetting the country. What is upsetting the country is a sense of its own identity. If, for example, one managed to change the curriculum in all the schools so that Negroes learned more about themselves and their real contributions to this culture, you would be liberating not only Negroes, you'd be liberating white people who know nothing about their own history. And the reason is that if you are compelled to lie about one aspect of anybody's history, you must lie about it all. If you have to lie about my real role here, if you have to pretend that I hoed all that cotton just because I loved you, then you have done something to yourself. You are mad.

Now let's go back a minute. I talked earlier about

those silent people—the porter and the maid—who, as I said, don't look up at the sky if you ask them if it is raining, but look into your face. My ancestors and I were very well trained. We understood very early that this was not a Christian nation. It didn't matter what you said or how often you went to church. My father and my mother and my grandfather and my grandmother knew that Christians didn't act this way. It was as simple as that. And if that was so there was no point in dealing with white people in terms of their own moral professions, for they were not going to honor them. What one did was to turn away, smiling all the time, and tell white people what they wanted to hear. But people always accuse you of reckless talk when you say this.

All this means that there are in this country tremendous reservoirs of bitterness which have never been able to find an outlet, but may find an outlet soon. It means that well-meaning white liberals place themselves in great danger when they try to deal with Negroes as though they were missionaries. It means, in brief, that a great price is demanded to liberate all those silent people so that they can breathe for the first time and *tell* you what they think of you. And a price is demanded to liberate all those white children—some of them near forty—who have never grown up, and who never will grow up, because they have no sense of their identity.

* * *

What passes for identity in America is a series of myths about one's heroic ancestors. It's astounding to me, for example, that so many people really appear to believe that the country was founded by a band of heroes who wanted to be free. That happens not to be true. What happened was that some people left Europe because they couldn't stay there any longer and had to go someplace else to make it. That's all. They were hungry, they were poor, they were convicts. Those who were making it in England, for example, did not get on the *Mayflower*.

That's how the country was settled. Not by Gary Cooper. Yet we have a whole race of people, a whole republic, who believe the myths to the point where even today they select them, and it shows in every level of national life. When I was living in Europe, for example, one of the worst revelations to me was the way Americans walked around Europe buying this and buying that and insulting everybody—not even out of malice, just because they didn't know any better. Well, that is the way they have always treated me. They weren't cruel, they just didn't know you were alive. They didn't know you had any feelings.

What I am trying to suggest here is that in the doing of all this for one hundred years or more, it is the American white man who has long since lost his grip on reality. In some peculiar way, having created this myth about Negroes, and the myth about his own history, he created myths about the world so that, for example, he was astounded that some people could prefer Castro, astounded that there are people in the world who don't go into hiding when they hear the word "Communism," astounded that Communism is one of the realities of the twentieth century which we will not overcome by pretending that it does not exist. The political level in this country now, on the part of people who should know better, is abysmal.

The Bible says somewhere that where there is no vision the people perish. I don't think anyone can doubt that in this country today we are menaced—intolerably menaced—by a lack of vision.

It is inconceivable that a sovereign people should continue, as we do so abjectly, to say, "I can't do anything about it. It's the government." The government is the creation of the people. It is responsible to the people. And the people are responsible for it. No American has the right to allow the present government to say, when Negro children are being bombed and hosed and shot and beaten all over the Deep South, that there is nothing we can do about it. There must have been a day in this country's life when the bombing of the children in Sunday School would have created a public uproar and endangered the life of a Governor Wallace. It happened here and there was no public uproar.

I began by saying that one of the paradoxes of education was that precisely at the point when you begin to develop a conscience, you must find yourself at war with your society. It is your responsibility to change society if you think of yourself as an educated person. And on the basis of the evidence—the moral and political evidence—one is compelled to say that this is a backward society. Now if I were a teacher in this school, or any Negro school, and I was dealing with Negro children, who were in my care only a few hours of every day and would then return to their homes and to the streets, children who have an apprehension of their future which with every hour grows grimmer and darker, I would try to teach them—I would try to make them know—that those streets, those houses, those dangers, those agonies by which they are surrounded, are criminal. I would try to make each child know that these things are the result of a criminal conspiracy to destroy him. I would teach him that if he intends to get to be a man, he must at once decide that he is stronger than this conspiracy and that he must never make his peace with it. And that one of his weapons for refusing to make his peace with it and for destroying it depends on what he decides he is worth. I would teach him that there are currently very few standards in this country which are worth a man's respect. That it is up to him to begin to change these standards for the sake of the life and the health of the country. I would suggest to him that the popular culture—as represented, for example, on television and in comic books and in movies—is based on fantasies created by very ill people, and he must be aware that these are fantasies that have nothing to do with reality. I would teach him that the press he reads is not as free as it says it is—and that he can do something about that, too. I would try to make him know that just as American history is longer, larger, more various, more beautiful, and more terrible than anything anyone has ever said about it, so is the world larger, more daring, more beautiful and more terrible, but principally larger—and that it belongs to him. I would teach him that he doesn't have to be bound by the expediencies of any given administration, any given policy, any given morality; that he has the right and the necessity to examine everything. I would try to show him that one has not learned anything about Castro when one says, "He is a Communist." This is a way of his learning something about Castro, something about Cuba, something, in time, about the world. I would suggest to him that he is living, at the moment, in an enormous province. America is not the world and if America is going to become a nation, she must find a way—and this child must help her to find a way to use the tremendous potential and tremendous energy which this child represents. If this country does not find a way to use that energy, it will be destroyed by that energy.

MARTIN LUTHER KING, JR.

"I HAVE A DREAM"

Martin Luther King, Jr. (1929–1968), was America's most influential African-American leader. A civil rights activist and preacher, he came into national prominence with the Montgomery, Alabama, bus boycott in 1955. It was the beginning of a career without parallel in America, one in which the young minister guided the Southern Christian Leadership Conference through a succession of nonviolent protests that led to legislation outlawing segregation in the nation.

King's eloquent pleas and noble cause for the rights of African Americans won the support of millions of people—blacks and whites—and made him an international figure of renown. He was awarded the 1964 Nobel Peace Prize for his courage and determination in leading nonviolent civil rights demonstrations throughout the nation.

One of the highlights of King's powerful influence was the historic March on Washington on August 28, 1963. More than 200,000 Americans assembled in the nation's capital at the Lincoln Memorial to demonstrate against civil wrongs and listen to civil rights leaders deplore the practices threatening the rights of African Americans. All spoke effectively, but none more so than Martin Luther King, Jr. His speech recognized the plight of being black in America, bound by poverty and hounded by discrimination. Charging America with this crime, King warned of the dissatisfaction of his people. But his dream was one of hope and salvation—hope for the nation, salvation for the American people.

FIVE SCORE YEARS AGO, a great American, in whose symbolic shadow we stand today, signed the Emancipation Proclamation. This momentous decree came as a great beacon of light of hope to millions of Negro slaves who had been seared in the flames of withering injustice. It came as a joyous daybreak to end the long night of their captivity.

But one hundred years later, the Negro still is not free. One hundred years later, the life of the Negro is still sadly crippled by the manacles of segregation and the chains of discrimination.

One hundred years later, the Negro lives on a lonely island of poverty in the midst of a vast ocean of material prosperity. One hundred years later, the Negro is still languished in the corners of American society and finds himself an exile in his own land. So we have come here today to dramatize a shameful condition.

In a sense we have come to our nation's capital to cash a check. When the architects of our republic wrote the magnificent words of the Constitution and the Declaration of Independence, they were signing a promissory note to which every American was to fall heir. This note was a promise that all men, yes, black men as well as white men, would be granted the unalienable rights of life, liberty, and the pursuit of happiness.

It is obvious today that America has defaulted on this promissory note insofar as her citizens of color are concerned. Instead of honoring this sacred obligation,

America has given the Negro people a bad check; which has come back marked "insufficient funds."

But we refuse to believe that the bank of justice is bankrupt. We refuse to believe that there are insufficient funds in the great vaults of opportunity of this nation. So we have come to cash this check—a check that will give us upon demand the riches of freedom and the security of justice.

We have also come to this hallowed spot to remind America of the fierce urgency of now. This is no time to engage in the luxury of cooling off or to take the tranquilizing drug of gradualism. Now is the time to make real the promises of democracy. Now is the time to rise from the dark and desolate valley of segregation to the sunlit path of racial justice. Now is time to lift our nation from the quick sands of racial injustice to the solid rock of brotherhood. Now is the time to make justice a reality for all of God's children.

It would be fatal for the nation to overlook the urgency of the movement and to underestimate the determination of the Negro. This sweltering summer of the Negro's legitimate discontent will not pass until there is an invigorating autumn of freedom and equality. 1963 is not an end but a beginning. Those who hope that the Negro needed to blow off steam and will now be content will have a rude awakening if the nation returns to business as usual.

There will be neither rest nor tranquility in America until the Negro is granted his citizenship rights. The whirlwinds of revolt will continue to shake the foundations of our nation until the bright day of justice emerges.

But there is something that I must say to my people who stand on the warm threshold which leads into the palace of justice. In the process of gaining our rightful place we must not be guilty of wrongful deeds.

Let us not seek to satisfy our thirst for freedom by drinking from the cup of bitterness and hatred. We must forever conduct our struggle on the high plane of dignity and discipline. We must not allow our creative protest to degenerate into physical violence. Again and again we must rise to the majestic heights of meeting physical force with soul force.

The marvelous new militancy which has engulfed the Negro community must not lead us to a distrust of all white people, for many of our white brothers, as evidenced by their presence here today, have come to realize that their destiny is tied up with our destiny and they have come to realize that their freedom is inextricably bound to our freedom. This offense we share mounted to storm the battlements of injustice must be carried forth by a bi-racial army. We cannot walk alone.

And as we walk, we must make the pledge that we shall always march ahead. We cannot turn back. There are those who are asking the devotees of civil rights, "When will you be satisfied?" We can never be satisfied as long as the Negro is the victim of the unspeakable horrors of police brutality.

We can never be satisfied as long as our bodies, heavy with the fatigue of travel, cannot gain lodging in the motels of the highways and the hotels of the cities. We cannot be satisfied as long as the Negro's basic mobility is from a smaller ghetto to a larger one.

We can never be satisfied as long as our children are stripped of their selfhood and robbed of their dignity by signs stating "for whites only." We cannot be satisfied as long as a Negro in Mississippi cannot vote and a Negro in New York believes he has nothing for which to vote. No, we are not satisfied, and we will not be satisfied until justice rolls down like waters and righteousness like a mighty stream.

I am not unmindful that some of you have come here out of excessive trials and tribulation. Some of you have come fresh from narrow jail cells. Some of you have come from areas where your quest for freedom left you battered by the storms of persecution and staggered by the winds of police brutality. You have been the veterans of creative suffering. Continue to work with the faith that unearned suffering is redemptive.

Go back to Mississippi; go back to Alabama; go back to South Carolina; go back to Georgia; go back to Louisiana; go back to the slums and ghettos of the Northern cities, knowing that somehow this situation can, and will be changed. Let us not wallow in the valley of despair.

So I say to you, my friends, that even though we must face the difficulties of today and tomorrow, I still have a dream. It is a dream deeply rooted in the American dream that one day this nation will rise up and live out the true meaning of its creed—we hold these truths to be self evident, that all men are created equal.

I have a dream that one day on the red hills of Georgia, sons of former slaves and sons of former slave-owners will be able to sit down together at the table of brotherhood.

I have a dream that one day, even the state of Mississippi, a state sweltering with the heat of injustice, sweltering with the heat of oppression, will be transformed into an oasis of freedom and justice.

I have a dream my four little children will one day live in a nation where they will not be judged by the color of their skin but by content of their character. I have a dream today!

I have a dream that one day, down in Alabama, with its vicious racists, with its governor having his lips dripping with the words of interposition and nullification, that one day, right there in Alabama, little black boys and black girls will be able to join hands with little white boys and white girls as sisters and brothers. I have a dream today!

I have a dream that one day every valley shall be exalted, every hill and mountain shall be made low, the rough places shall be made plain, and the crooked places shall be made straight and the glory of the Lord will be revealed and all flesh shall see it together.

This is our hope. This is the faith that I go back to the South with.

With this faith we will be able to hear out of the mountain of despair a stone of hope. With this faith we will be able to transform the jangling discords of our nation into a beautiful symphony of brotherhood.

With this faith we will be able to work together to pray together, to struggle together, to go to jail together, to stand up for freedom together, knowing that we will be free one day. This will be the day when all of God's children will be able to sing with new meaning—"my country 'tis of thee; sweet land of liberty; of thee I sing; land where my fathers died, land of the pilgrim's pride; from every mountain side, let freedom ring"—and if America is to be a great nation, this must become true.

So let freedom ring from the prodigious hilltops of New Hampshire.

Let freedom ring from the mighty mountains of New York.

Let freedom ring from the heightening Alleghenies of Pennsylvania.

Let freedom ring from the snow-capped Rockies of Colorado.

Let freedom ring from the curvaceous slopes of California.

But not only that.

Let freedom ring from Stone Mountain of Georgia.

Let freedom ring from Lookout Mountain of Tennessee.

Let freedom ring from every hill and molehill of Mississippi, from every mountainside, let freedom ring.

And when we allow freedom to ring, when we let it ring from every village and hamlet, from every state and city, we will be able to speed up that day when all of God's children—black men and white men, Jews and Gentiles, Catholics and Protestants—will be able to join hands and to sing in the words of the old Negro spiritual. "Free at last, free at last; thank God Almighty, we are free at last."

MALCOLM X

"ADDRESS TO MISSISSIPPI YOUTH"

Malcolm X (1925–1965) was a radical leader with a revolutionary cause: to change a system of racial suppression, by violence if necessary. The germ of this idea was formed long before it became a conscious plan. Malcolm Little was the son of a militant Baptist clergyman who was murdered—possibly by members of a racist group like the Ku Klux Klan. By his late teens, young Malcolm had become a petty criminal. He was caught and sentenced to prison, where he studied religion and converted to the Muslim faith. He also changed his name to Malcolm X. After getting out of prison, he soon rose to the number-two position in the Nation of Islam.

In 1964, he quit the Nation of Islam and established a Muslim mosque and the Organization of Afro-American Unity, a black protest organization. Although he was to shift from a position of hatred of whites to the cause of black liberation, the voice of Malcolm X remained a force to be reckoned with by blacks and whites alike.

On December 31, 1964, he gave a speech to a delegation of thirty-seven teenagers at the Hotel Theresa in New York City. The group, sponsored by the Student Nonviolent Coordinating Committee (SNCC), was being rewarded with a vacation trip for their leadership roles in the civil rights struggle in their hometown of McComb, Mississippi. In his speech, Malcolm X encouraged his young audience of African Americans to think for themselves, to recognize their racial enemies, and to be assured that they were not alone in standing up to these enemies. The following is an excerpt from that speech.

ONE OF THE first things I think young people, especially nowadays, should learn is how to see for yourself and listen for yourself and think for yourself. If you form the habit of going by what you hear others say about someone, or going by what others think about someone, instead of searching that thing out for yourself and seeing for yourself, you will be walking west when you think you're going east, and you will be walking east when you think you're going west. This generation, especially of our people, has a burden, more so than any other time in history. The most important thing we can learn to do today is think for ourselves.

It's good to keep wide-open ears and listen to what everybody else has to say, but when you come to make decisions, you have to weigh all of what you've heard on its own, and place it where it belongs, and come to a decision for yourself; you'll never regret it. But if you form the habit of taking what someone else says about a thing without checking it out for yourself, you'll find that other people will have you hating your friends and loving your enemies. This is one of the things that our people are beginning to learn today—that it is very important to think out a situation for yourself. If you don't do it, you'll always be maneuvered into a situation where you are never fighting your actual enemies, where you will find yourself fighting your own self.

I think our people in this country are the best examples of that. Many of us want to be nonviolent and we talk very loudly, you know, about being nonviolent. Here in Harlem, where there are probably more black people concentrated than any place in the world, some talk that nonviolent talk too. But we find that they aren't nonviolent with each other. You can go out to Harlem Hospital, where there are more black patients than any hospital in the world, and see them going in there all cut up and shot up and busted up where they got violent with each other.

My experience has been that in many instances where you find Negroes talking about nonviolence, they are not nonviolent with each other, and they're not loving with each other, or forgiving with each other. Usually when they say they're nonviolent, they mean they're nonviolent with somebody else. I think you understand what I mean. They are nonviolent with the enemy. A person can come to your home, and if he's white and wants to heap some kind of brutality on you, you're nonviolent; or he can come to take your father and put a rope around his neck and you're nonviolent. But if another Negro just stomps his foot, you'll rumble with him in a minute. Which shows you that there's an inconsistency there.

If the leaders of the nonviolent movement can go into the white community and teach nonviolence, good. I'd go along with that. But as long as I see them teaching nonviolence only in the black community, we can't go along with that. We believe in equality, and equality means that you have to put the same thing over here that you put over there. And if black people alone are going to be the ones who are nonviolent, then it's not fair. We throw ourselves off guard. In fact, we disarm ourselves and make ourselves defenseless.

I think in 1965—whether you like it, or I like it, or they like it, or not—you will see that there is a generation of black people becoming mature to the point where they feel that they have no more business being asked to take a peaceful approach than anybody else has, unless everybody's going to take a peaceful approach.

So we here in the Organization of Afro-American Unity are with the struggle in Mississippi one thousand percent. We're with the efforts to register our people in Mississippi to vote one thousand percent. But we do not go along with anybody telling us to help nonviolently. We think that if the government says that Negroes have a right to vote, and then some Negroes come out to vote, and some kind of Ku Klux Klan is going to put them in the river, and the government doesn't do anything about it, it's time for us to organize and band together and equip ourselves and qualify ourselves to protect ourselves. And once you can protect yourself, you don't have to worry about being hurt.

That doesn't mean we're against white people, but we sure are against the Ku Klux Klan and the White Citizens Councils; and anything that looks like it's against us, we're against it. Excuse me for raising my voice, but this thing, you know, gets me upset. Imagine that—a country that's supposed to be a democracy, supposed to be for freedom and all of that kind of stuff when they want to draft you and put you in the Army and send you to Saigon to fight for them—and then you've got to turn around and all night long discuss how you're going to just get a right to register and vote without being murdered. Why, that's the most hypocritical government since the world began!

I hope you don't think I'm trying to incite you. Just look here: Look at yourselves. Some of you are teen-agers, students. How do you think I feel—and I belong to a generation ahead of you—how do you think I feel to have to tell you, "We, my generation, sat around like a knot on a wall while the whole world was fighting for its human rights—and you've got to be born into a society where you still have the same fight." What did we do, who preceded you? I'll tell you what we did: Nothing. And don't you make the same mistake we made.

You get freedom by letting your enemy know that you'll do anything to get your freedom; then you'll get it. It's the only way you'll get it. When you get that kind of attitude, they'll label you as a "crazy Negro," or they'll call you a "crazy nigger"—they don't say Negro. Or they'll call you an extremist or a subversive, or seditious, or a red or a radical. But when you stay radical long enough, and get enough people to be like you, you'll get your freedom.

So don't you run around here trying to make friends with somebody who's depriving you of your rights. They're not your friends, no, they're your enemies. Treat them like that and fight them, and you'll get your freedom: and after you get your freedom, your enemy will respect you. And we'll respect you. And I say that with no hate. I don't have hate in me. I have no hate at all. I don't have any hate. I've got some sense. I'm not going to let somebody who hates me tell me to love him. I'm not that way-out. And you, young as you are, and because you start thinking, you're not going to do it either. The only time you're going to get in that bag is if somebody puts you there. Somebody else, who doesn't have your welfare at heart.

"STOKELY CARMICHAEL ON BLACK POWER"

As head of the Student Nonviolent Coordinating Committee (SNCC), Stokely Carmichael (1941–   ) was a leading
force in the civil rights revolution of the 1960s. He is
credited with originating the expression "Black Power."

As exaggerated by the news media in giant headlines
and frequent broadcasts, the term took on dangerous
meaning, and Black Power became a code phrase for black
racism, racial hatred, violence, and separation. But by
"Black Power," Carmichael meant the end of white supremacy, the beginning of black integrity, and recognition
of black Americans by white Americans. Toward this end,
he called for black political and economic action.

The following is an excerpt from a speech Carmichael
made on November 16, 1966, at the University of California at Berkeley. In his address, Carmichael points out
why racism can no longer be ignored and its abuse of
African Americans no longer tolerated.

IT SEEMS TO ME that the institutions that function in this
country are clearly racist, and that they're built upon

racism. And the question then is, how can black people inside this country move? And then how can white people, who say they're not a part of those institutions, begin to move, and how then do we begin to clear away the obstacles that we have in this society that keep us from living like human beings. How can we begin to build institutions that will allow people to relate with each other as human beings? This country has never done that. Especially around the concept of white or black.

Now several people have been upset because we've said that integration was irrelevant when initiated by blacks and that in fact it was a subterfuge, an insidious subterfuge for the maintenance of white supremacy. We maintain that in the past six years or so this country has been feeding us a thalidomide drug of integration, and that some Negroes have been walking down a dream street talking about sitting next to white people, and that that does not begin to solve the problem. When we went to Mississippi, we did not go to sit next to Ross Barnett; we did not go to sit next to Jim Clark; we went to get them out of our way, and people ought to understand that. We were never fighting for the right to integrate, we were fighting against white supremacy. . . .

Now we are engaged in a psychological struggle in this country and that struggle is whether or not black people have the right to use the words they want to use without white people giving their sanction to it. We maintain, whether they like it or not, we gon' use the word "black power" and let them address themselves to that. We are not gonna wait for white people to sanction black power. We're tired of waiting. Every time black people move in this country, they're forced to defend their position before they move. It's time that the people who're supposed to be defending their position do that. That's white people. They ought to start defending themselves, as to why they have oppressed and exploited us.

It is clear that when this country started to move in

terms of slavery, the reason for a man being picked as a slave was one reason: because of the color of his skin. If one was black one was automatically inferior, inhuman, and therefore fit for slavery. So that the question of whether or not we are individually suppressed is nonsensical and is a downright lie. We are oppressed as a group because we are black, not because we are lazy, not because we're apathetic, not because we're stupid, not because we smell, not because we eat watermelon and have good rhythm. We are oppressed because we are black, and in order to get out of that oppression, one must feel the group power that one has. Not the individual power which this country then sets the criteria under which a man may come into it. That is what is called in this country as integration. You do what I tell you to do, and then we'll let you sit at the table with us. And then we are saying that we have to be opposed to that. We must now set a criteria, and that if there's going to be any integration it's going to be a two-way thing. If you believe in integration, you can come live in Watts. You can send your children to the ghetto schools. Let's talk about that. If you believe in integration, then we're going to start adopting us some white people to live in our neighborhood. So it is clear that the question is not one of integration or segregation. Integration is a man's ability to want to move in there by himself. If someone wants to live in a white neighborhood and he is black, that is his choice. It should be his right. It is not because white people will allow him. So vice-versa, if a black man wants to live in the slums, that should be his right. Black people will let him, that is the difference.

It is this difference which points up the logical mistakes this country makes when it begins to criticize the program articulated by SNCC. We maintain that we cannot afford to be concerned about 6 percent of the children in this country. I mean the black children who you allow to come into white schools. We have 94 percent who still live in shacks. We are going to be concerned about those 94 percent. You ought to be concerned about them, too. The question is, are we willing to be concerned about those 94 percent. Are we willing to be concerned about the black people who will never get to Berkeley, who will never get to Harvard and cannot get an education, so you'll never get a chance to rub shoulders with them and say, "Well he's almost as good as we are; he's not like the others." The question is, how can white society begin to move to see black people as human beings? I am black, therefore I am. Not that I am black and I must go to college to prove myself. I am black, therefore I am. And don't surprise me with anything and say to me that you must go to college before you gain access to X, Y, and Z. It is only a rationalization for one's oppression.

The political parties in this country do not meet the needs of the people on a day-to-day basis. The question is, how can we build new political institutions that will become the political expressions of people on a day-to-day basis. The question is, how can you build political institutions that will begin to meet the needs of Oakland, California; and the needs of Oakland, California is not 1,000 policemen with submachine guns. They don't need that. They need that least of all. The question is, how can we build institutions where those people can begin to function on a day-to-day basis, where they can get decent jobs, where they can get decent housing, and where they can begin to participate in the policy and major decisions that affect their lives. That's what they need. Not Gestapo troops. Because this is not 1942. And if you play like Nazis, we're playing back with you this time around. Get hip to that.

The question then is, how can white people move to start making the major institutions that they have in this country function the way they are supposed to function? That is the real question. And can white people move inside their own community and start tearing down racism where, in fact, it does exist? It is you who live in Cicero and stop us from living there. It is white people who stop us from moving into Grenada. It is white people who make sure that we live in the ghettos of this country. It is white institutions that do that. They must change. In order for America to really live on a basic principle of human relationships, a new society must be born. Racism must die, and the economic exploitation of this country, of non-white people around the world, must also die. . . .

SHIRLEY CHISHOLM

"THE BUSINESS OF AMERICA IS WAR, AND IT IS TIME FOR A CHANGE"

Shirley Chisholm (1924–   ) was elected to Congress in 1964 from the heavily populated black community of Bedford Stuyvesant in Brooklyn, New York. A proven veteran of local political battles, she had had five years' experience in the New York State Assembly. During that time she earned the name "Fighting Shirley Chisholm," and was well prepared for the political battles waiting in the House of Representatives.

As the first female African-American member of Congress, she looked forward to serving on a committee that dealt with the problems of people in her community. Instead, she was assigned to the House Agricultural Subcommittee on Forestry and Rural Villages. Protesting that nothing could be further from her interest and experience, she managed to be reassigned to the Veterans Affairs Committee.

Chisholm was disappointed but far from discouraged, as she made clear in her first speech before the House of

Representatives, delivered on March 16, 1969. Most of that speech follows.

MR. SPEAKER, on the same day President Nixon announced he had decided the United States will not be safe unless we start to build a defense system against missiles, the Headstart program in the District of Columbia was cut back for the lack of money.

As a teacher, and as a woman, I do not think I will ever understand what kind of values can be involved in spending nine billion dollars—and more, I am sure—on elaborate, unnecessary and impractical weapons when several thousand disadvantaged children in the nation's capital get nothing.

When the new administration took office, I was one of the many Americans who hoped it would mean that our country would benefit from the fresh perspectives, the new ideas, the different priorities of a leader who had no part in the mistakes of the past. Mr. Nixon had said things like this:

"If our cities are to be livable for the next generation, we can delay no longer in launching new approaches to the problems that beset them and to the tensions that tear them apart."

And he said, "When you cut expenditures for education, what you are doing is shortchanging the American future."

But frankly, I have never cared too much what people say. What I am interested in is what they do. We have waited to see what the new administration is going to do. The pattern now is becoming clear.

Apparently launching those new programs can be delayed for a while, after all. It seems we have to get some missiles launched first. . . .

The new Secretary of Health, Education and Welfare, Robert Finch, came to the Hill to tell the House Education and Labor Committee that he thinks we should spend more on education, particularly in city schools. But, he said, unfortunately we cannot "afford" to, until we have reached some kind of honorable solution to the Vietnam war. I was glad to read that the distinguished Member from Oregon asked Mr. Finch this:

"With the crisis we have in education, and the crisis in our cities, can we wait to settle the war? Shouldn't it be the other way around? Unless we can meet the crisis in education, we really can't afford the war."

Secretary of Defense Melvin Laird came to Capitol Hill, too. His mission was to sell the antiballistic-missile insanity to the Senate. . . . Mr. Laird talked of being prepared to spend at least two more years in Vietnam.

Two more years, two more years of hunger for Americans, of death for our best young men, of children here at home suffering the lifelong handicap of not having a good education when they are young. Two more years of high taxes, collected to feed the cancerous growth of a Defense Department budget that now consumes two thirds of our federal income.

Two more years of too little being done to fight our greatest enemies, poverty, prejudice and neglect, here in our own country. Two more years of fantastic waste in the Defense Department and of penny pinching on social programs. Our country cannot survive two more years, or four, of these kinds of policies. It must stop—this year— now.

Now, I am not a pacifist. I am deeply, unalterably opposed to this war in Vietnam. Apart from all the other considerations—and they are many—the main fact is that we cannot squander there the lives, the money, the energy that we need desperately here, in our cities, in our schools.

I wonder whether we cannot reverse our whole approach to spending. For years, we have given the military, the defense industry, a blank check. New weapons systems are dreamed up, billions are spent, and many times they are found to be impractical, inefficient, unsatisfactory, even worthless. What do we do then? We spend more money on them. But with social programs, what do we do? Take the Job Corps. Its failure has been mercilessly exposed and criticized. If it had been a military research and development project, they would have been covered up or explained away, and Congress would have been ready to pour more billions after those that had been wasted on it.

The case of Pride, Inc., is interesting. This vigorous, successful black organization, here in Washington, conceived and built by young inner-city men, has been ruthlessly attacked by its enemies in the government, in this Congress. At least six auditors from the General Accounting Office were put to work investigating Pride. They worked seven months and spent more than $100,000. They uncovered a fraud. It was something less than $2,100. Meanwhile, millions of dollars—billions of dollars, in fact—were being spent by the Department of Defense, and how many auditors and investigators were checking into their negotiated contracts? Five.

We Americans have come to feel that it is our mission to make the world free. We believe that we are the good guys, everywhere—in Vietnam, in Latin America, wherever we go. We believe we are the good guys at home, too. When the Kerner Commission told white America what black America had always known, that prejudice and hatred built the nation's slums, maintain them and profit by them, white America would not believe it. But it is true. Unless we start to fight and defeat the enemies of poverty and racism in our own country and make our talk of equality and opportunity ring true, we are exposed as hypocrites in the eyes of the world when we talk about making other people free.

I am deeply disappointed at the clear evidence that the number-one priority of the new administration is to buy more and more weapons of war, to return to the era

of the cold war, to ignore the war we must fight here—
the war that is not optional. There is only one way, I
believe, to turn these policies around. The Congress can
respond to the mandate that the American people have
clearly expressed. They have said, "End this war. Stop
the waste. Stop the killing. Do something for your own
people first." We must find the money to "launch the new
approaches," as Mr. Nixon said. We must force the administration to rethink its distorted, unreal scale of priorities.
Our children, our jobless men, our deprived, rejected and
starving fellow citizens must come first.

For this reason, I intend to vote "No" on every money
bill that comes to the floor of this House that provides
any funds for the Department of Defense. Any bill what-
soever, until the time comes when our values and priorities have been turned right side up again, until the
monstrous waste and the shocking profits in the defense
budget have been eliminated and our country starts to
use its strength, its tremendous resources, for people and
peace, not for profits and war.

It was Calvin Coolidge, I believe, who made the comment that "the Business of America is Business." We are
now spending eighty billion dollars a year on defense—
that is two thirds of every tax dollar. At this time, gentlemen, the business of America is war, and it is time for a
change.

JAMES FORMAN

"BLACK MANIFESTO"

James Forman (1929–) was executive secretary of the Student Nonviolent Coordinating Committee (SNCC) at the height of the civil rights revolution, when members of this African-American organization were arrested by the thousands for their active efforts to encourage voter registration.

On April 26, 1969, Forman delivered a speech at the National Black Economic Development Conference in Detroit, Michigan. His presentation marked the first large-scale claim that African Americans were due reparations—that is, repayment for damages done in the past. Those damages had been done during the years African Americans were forced to perform free labor under the slave system, and the years of deprivation ever since.

Forman called his presentation the "Black Manifesto." He demanded that white churches and synagogues pay five hundred million dollars to help African Americans develop communications skills, and establish a labor strike and defense fund, a Southern land bank, and a

United Black Appeal to set up cooperative business. "We must commit ourselves to a society where the total means of production are taken from the rich people and placed into the hands of the state for the welfare of all the people," Forman said in the speech that follows.

BROTHERS AND SISTERS:

We have come from all over the country, burning with anger and despair not only with the miserable economic plight of our people, but fully aware that the racism on which the Western world was built dominates our lives. There can be no separation of the problems of racism from the problems of our economic, political, and cultural degradation. To any black man, this is clear.

But there are still some of our people who are clinging to the rhetoric of the Negro and we must separate ourselves from those Negroes who go around the country promoting all types of schemes for black capitalism.

Ironically, some of the most militant black nationalists, as they call themselves, have been the first to jump on the bandwagon of black capitalism. They are pimps: Black Power Pimps and fraudulent leaders and the people must be educated to understand that any black man or Negro who is advocating a perpetuation of capitalism inside the United States is in fact seeking not only his ultimate destruction and death, but is contributing to the continuous exploitation of black people all around the world. For it is the power of the United States Government, this racist, imperialist government, that is choking the life of all people around the world.

We are an African people. We sit back and watch the Jews in this country make Israel a powerful conservative state in the Middle East, but we are not concerned actively about the plight of our brothers in Africa. We are the most advanced technological group of black people in the world, and there are many skills that could be offered to Africa. At the same time, it must be publicly stated that many African leaders are in disarray themselves, having been duped into following the lines as laid out by the Western imperialist governments.

Africans themselves succumbed to and are victims of the power of the United States. For instance, during the summer of 1967, as the representatives of SNCC, Howard Moore and I traveled extensively in Tanzania and Zambia. We talked to high, very high, government officials. We told them there were many black people in the United States who were willing to come and work in Africa. All these government officials who were part of the leadership in their respective governments, said they wanted us to send as many skilled people as we could contact. But this program never came into fruition and we do not know the exact reason, for I assure you that we talked and were committed to making this a successful program. It is our guess that the United States put the squeeze on these countries, for such a program directed by SNCC would have been too dangerous to the international prestige of the U.S. It is also possible that some of the wild statements by some black leaders frightened the Africans.

In Africa today, there is a great suspicion of black people in this country. This is a correct suspicion since most of the Negroes who have left the States for work in Africa usually work for the Central Intelligence Agency (CIA) or the State Department. But the respect for us as a people continues to mount and the day will come when we can return to our homeland as brothers and sisters. But we should not think of going to Africa today, for we are located in a strategic position. We live inside the United States, which is the most barbaric country in the world and we have a chance to help bring this government down.

Time is short and we do not have much time and it is time we stop mincing words. Caution is fine, but no oppressed people ever gained their liberation until they were ready to fight, to use whatever means necessary, including the use of force and power of the gun to bring down the colonizer.

We have heard the rhetoric, but we have not heard the rhetoric which says that black people in this country must understand that we are the Vanguard Force. We shall liberate all the people in the United States and we will be instrumental in the liberation of colored people the world around. We must understand this point very clearly so that we are not trapped into diversionary and reactionary movements. Any class analysis of the United States shows very clearly that black people are the most oppressed group of people inside the United States. We have suffered the most from racism and exploitation, cultural degradation and lack of political power. It follows from the laws of revolution that the most oppressed will make the revolution. All the parties on the left who consider themselves revolutionary will say that blacks are the Vanguard, but we are saying that not only are we the Vanguard, but we must assume leadership, total control and we must exercise the humanity which is inherent in us. We are the most humane people within the United States. We have suffered and we understand suffering. Our hearts go out to the Vietnamese for we know what it is to suffer under the domination of racist America. Our hearts, our souls and all the compassion we can mount goes out to our brothers in Africa, Santo Domingo, Latin America and Asia who are being tricked by the power structure of the United States, which is dominating the world today. These ruthless, barbaric men have systematically tried to kill all people and organizations opposed to its imperialism. We no longer can just get by with the use of the word capitalism to describe the United States, for it is an imperial power, sending money, missionaries and the army throughout the world to protect this government and the few rich whites who control it. General Motors and all the major auto industries are operating in South Africa, yet the white dominated leadership of the United Auto Workers sees no relationship to the exploitation of black people in South Africa and the exploitation of black people in the United States. If they understand it, they certainly do not put it into practice, which is the actual test. We as black people must be concerned with the total conditions of all black people in the world.

But while we talk of revolution, which will be an armed confrontation and long years of sustained guerrilla warfare inside this country, we must also talk of the type of world we want to live in. We must commit ourselves to a society where the total means of production are taken from the rich people and placed into the hands of the state for the welfare of all the people. That is what we mean when we say total control. And we mean that black people who have suffered the most from exploitation and racism must move to protect their black interest by assuming leadership inside of the United States of everything that exists. The time has passed when we are second in command and the white boy stands on top. This is especially true of the Welfare Agencies in this country, but it is not enough to say that a black man is on top. He must be committed to building the new society, to taking the wealth away from the rich people such as General Motors, Ford, Chrysler, the DuPonts, the Rockefellers, the Mellons, and all the other rich white exploiters and racists who run this world.

Where do we begin? We have already started. We started the moment we were brought to this country. In fact, we started on the shores of Africa, for we have always resisted attempts to make us slaves and now we must resist the attempts to make us capitalists. It is in the financial interest of the United States to make us capitalists, for this will be the same line as that of integration into the main-stream of American life. Therefore, brothers and sisters, there is no need to fall into the trap that we have to get an ideology. We have an ideology. Our fight is against racism, capitalism and imperialism and we are dedicated to building a socialist society inside the United States where the total means of production and distribution are in the hands of the State and that must be led by black people, by revolutionary blacks who are concerned about the total humanity of this world. And, therefore, we obviously are different from some of those who seek a black nation in the United States, for there is no way for the nation to be viable, if in fact the United States remains in the hands of white racists. Then, too, let us deal with some arguments that we should share power with whites. We say that there must be a revolutionary black Vanguard and that white people in this country must be willing to accept black leadership, for that is the only protection that black people have to protect ourselves from racism rising again in this country.

Racism in the U.S. is so pervasive in the mentality of whites that only an armed, well-disciplined, black-controlled government can insure the stamping out of racism in this country. And that is why we plead with black people not to be talking about a few crumbs, a few thousand dollars for this cooperative, or a thousand dollars which splits black people into fighting over the dollar. That is the intention of the government. We say . . . think in terms of total control of the United States. Prepare ourselves to seize state power. Do not hedge, for time is short and all around the world, the forces of liberation are directing their attacks against the United States. It is a powerful country, but that power is not greater than that of black people. We work the chief industries in this country and we could cripple the economy while the brothers fought guerrilla warfare in the streets. This will take some long-range planning, but whether it happens in a thousand years is of no consequence. It cannot happen unless we start. How then is all of this related to this conference?

First of all, this conference is called by a set of religious people, Christians who have been involved in the exploitation and rape of black people since the country was founded. The missionary goes hand in hand with the power of the states. We must begin seizing power wherever we are and we must say to the planners of this conference that you are no longer in charge. We the people who have assembled here thank you for getting us here, but we are going to assume power over the conference and determine from this moment on the direction in which we want it to go. We are not saying that the conference was planned badly. The staff of the conference has worked hard and has done a magnificent job in bringing all of us together and we must include them in the new leadership which must surface from this point on. The conference is now the property of the people who are assembled here. This we proclaim as fact and not rhetoric and there are demands that we are going to make and we insist that the planners of this conference help us implement them.

We maintain we have the revolutionary right to do this. We have the same rights, if you will, as the Christians had in going to Africa and raping our Motherland and bringing us away from our continent of peace and into this hostile and alien environment where we have been living in perpetual warfare since 1619.

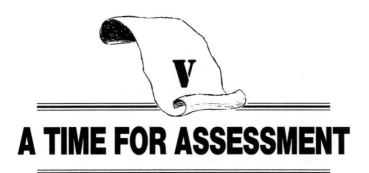

A TIME FOR ASSESSMENT

The achievement of the 1960s was in the long, historic struggle of African Americans to gain an equality of opportunity. With the support of new laws to back their demands, African Americans were to learn the difference between rules and regulations, and the racial discrimination practiced by people. The 1970s and 1980s were clearly times of review and evaluation, times for African Americans to understand what remained to be done.

Various organizations watched to see that civil rights laws were being enforced. The benefit of this vigilance was nowhere more productive than in voter registration. As a result, more African Americans were elected to public offices than at any time since Reconstruction.

Despite legislation supporting equality of job opportunity, however, companies continued to discriminate against minorities in hiring. Unions remained a major offender. These largest organizations of industrial workers safeguarded the employment interest of their members. But their membership was hardly representative of the thousands of African Americans working in industry.

And education continued to function as a racially separate and unequal system in fact, if not by law. This was particularly true in black ghettos throughout the United States. The result left black youngsters ill prepared to compete with white youngsters, a condition that held little promise of change for them as adults. Nevertheless, their spirit remained intact. This fact was a saving grace, deserving of all the efforts yet needed for continued change and improvement.

VERNON F. JORDAN, JR.

"BLACK PEOPLE AND THE UNIONS"

Skilled craftspeople have always been respected for the quality of their work. After the founding of America, many African Americans were to share with white Americans in this proud tradition. As the number of white practitioners grew, they organized into unions and barred black artisans from membership. And only union members were hired in skilled trades. Black artisans were left out with no place to work.

This system of unions favoring friends and relatives has continued to this day. It denies most African Americans and other minorities the opportunity to work in the high-paying jobs provided by the skilled trades.

Nepotism in the trades was the subject of an address by Vernon F. Jordan, Jr. (1935–) at the national American Federation of Labor–Congress of Industrial Organizations (AFL-CIO) convention in Miami on November 22, 1971. Jordan spoke as the newly appointed executive director of the National Urban League, a position he held until 1981, when he went into private law practice. A civil rights leader, he is a graduate of Howard University Law School and has worked for an Atlanta civil rights lawyer. He has led boycotts and served as director of the Voter Education Project of the Southern Regional Council. He was serving as executive director of the United Negro College Fund when he was named to head the Urban League.

IN THE SIXTIES, we were fighting for our rights, which we tore from a reluctant nation. In the sixties, the burning issue was whether blacks would be allowed to ride the busses and where they would sit. In the seventies, the issues have shifted. Now the issues are whether black people will be allowed to drive that bus, whether the masses of black people will have the money to pay the fare, whether blacks have their rightful place as executives and directors of the bus company and the unions it deals with, and whether the bus routes will link the black ghetto to where the jobs are.

The issue of the day is, then, the economic empowerment of black people. This is the task to which we of the Urban League have committed ourselves, and it is the task which the labor movement, of all the partners in the coalition for justice in America, should find the most congenial to its special talents and interests.

I would like to discuss with you today the goals of black Americans, the nature of the coalition strategy, and the specific role I see for the labor movement, in joint action with black people, in bringing an end to poverty, joblessness and hardship in this nation of unprecedented wealth and power.

It goes without saying that the goal of black Americans is for total, unconditional and complete equality. For too long have we been excluded from parity with white Americans. For too long have we been victims of racism and discrimination.

We want a share of the America we've fought and died for. We want our fair share of the jobs, the income, the opportunities and the political representation our numbers call for. The media has thrown a sharp spotlight on the blacks running for major offices around the country, but did you know that black people, who make up 12 per cent of the population, hold only three-tenths of one per cent of all the elective offices at local, state and federal levels of government?

The Black Caucus has received considerable press attention because of its forthright uncompromising position in favor of black people and working people. But are you aware that the Congressional Black Caucus comprises only three per cent of the House of Representatives?

Much—too much—has been made of the economic gains blacks have made in the past decade. Somehow, we are supposed to be overjoyed that we've finally achieved 61 per cent of white income or that the numbers of black families making over $10,000 have tripled or that the numbers of blacks attending college or holding professional and managerial jobs has increased.

But did you know that the dollar gap between whites and blacks has actually grown? In 1960 $2,600 separated the median black family income from white; in 1970, the dollar gap grew to $3,800. Did you know that the percentage of white families making over $10,000 is double the percentage of black families in that bracket? Are you aware that it takes three workers in a black family to make as much as one worker in the average white family? Or that black college graduates still average lower incomes than whites who never attended college? Or that blacks still have far less than our fair share of the top-dollar, top-status jobs while we continue to be disproportionately concentrated in lower-paying occupations?

About the only area where we have more than our fair share of the opportunities is poverty and unemployment.

We are not eleven per cent of the nation's poor; we are thirty per cent. We are not eleven percent of the unemployed, we are twenty per cent.

Through our goal of economic empowerment of black people, we seek to turn those figures around and achieve parity with other citizens of this nation whose skin is white, whose opportunities have not been withheld, and whose progress has been steady.

And we seek to do this through active alliances and coalitions with those elements of our society whose actions and ideals are consistent with ours, whose interests are similar and who share our commitment to a society that is just, a society that is fair, and a society that is decent.

One of the prerequisites of such coalitions is honesty. The partners must deal with each other from positions of equality and mutual respect. At times, they will say things that hurt, but it is far better for such feelings to be out in the open, freely discussed and dealt with, than to be festering beneath the surface, only to explode later.

It is in this spirit of mutual respect and the honesty our coalition demands, that I must call to your attention the deep frustration and suspicions some black people have of the labor movement. These feelings are entirely due to the racially restrictive practices of a handful of unions.

I refuse to magnify the wrongdoings of a few unions and thus join those who are the real enemies of black people, poor people, and working people. I recognize that the AFL-CIO and the labor movement in general is the home of some of the most progressive elements in American life, and is the beneficiary of the loyalty of black workers.

Black workers do not question the value of the union card; it is universally acknowledged to be a passport to economic freedom. In fact, a higher proportion of black workers than white are unionized. Blacks are 13 per cent of all union members. But because of restrictive practices, proportionately twice as many white construction craftsmen as blacks are organized. Where blacks are permitted to enter construction unions—primarily in the lower-skilled categories—a higher percentage of blacks are union members than are white. The payoff is in the paycheck. Wages of black construction craftsmen who have managed to enter unions average forty per cent higher than the wages of those who have not.

The existence of large numbers of unorganized black construction tradesmen can ultimately work to the disadvantage of the unions, in that they represent a temptation to throw more business to non-union contractors, they represent a constant threat of dual unionism, and their continued exclusion serves as a ripe excuse for anti-union forces within our society. Finally, the public image of the entire labor movement is unfairly harmed because of the continued practices of a small part of it.

I know that your leadership is working hard on this problem. I know that the Urban League and other groups are cooperating with many unions in the joint efforts to increase the numbers of black craftsmen and apprentices. And I am pleased that the Urban League has made progress with some construction unions. But in all candor I must say it is too little and too slow, in the face of what remains to be done. In the fraternal spirit of our mutual interests in economic justice, in the recognition that change must come from within, and in the conviction that deeds, not resolutions are called for, I ask this convention to intensify the pressures upon your backward brothers and raise them to the moral and pragmatic standards the rest of the labor movement follows.

First, we must organize the unorganized. The AFL-CIO has already done great work in helping farm workers, hospital workers, and sanitation workers win the right of union recognition. But in some instances it was the workers themselves who first organized unions, and then received assistance from the labor movement. I ask you to reverse that process: to place an even greater emphasis and impetus on bringing the benefits of unionism to the underpaid, exploited and poverty-stricken laboring men and women of America.

To an alarming degree, blacks and minorities are disproportionately represented among the unorganized poor. We read much about the shift to a service economy and the lack of growth in manufacturing. But what does this service economy mean to the labor movement? It is more than growth in the numbers of doctors, lawyers, and other professional service occupations. It means growing numbers of laundry workers, sanitation men, day care center workers, paraprofessional aides, domestics, and many other categories of workers whose wages are low, employment uncertain and prospects dim. In the South especially, black and white workers outside the union umbrella are vulnerable to the pressures of local land barons and repressive petty dictators.

The labor movement has demonstrated that it can deliver, and now it is charged to deliver its benefits to the masses of the unorganized. The need cannot be taken lightly. There is hunger in this land. There is abject poverty in our country. There is deep suffering in the urban ghettos and in the rural shacks of America. There is every bit as much of an emergency now as in the Depression, when unions organized similarly disadvantaged industrial workers. You got the Wagner Act to breathe life into your claims for justice; I now ask you to formulate an "AFL-CIO Act" to breathe life into the crying need for justice of today's unorganized laboring masses. Only you have the energy, the resources, and the expertise to do it.

Second: there is a need for greater numbers of blacks in union leadership roles. This is something that the Urban League with your cooperation and backing has encouraged. There are thousands of young budding Phil Randolphs all across the country, men and women who have been steeled in the struggle for civil rights to recognize the need for social justice and the benefits of unionism. A movement-wide campaign to identify, train and place this cadre of energetic unionists in positions of leadership within the labor movement will pay off in an internal strengthening of the movement and in the recognition among all black people that the union movement is indeed a progressive joining together of black and white workers for the benefit of all.

Third: I would urge you to expand your very valuable political education programs to make an even greater impact upon the black community. Here too, the Urban League stands ready and willing to join with you. In the coming months, we will be announcing a new program of voter registration and education in northern and western cities. Black people and poor people are underregistered. They are still kept from the ballot box by restrictive practices and by an unwritten desire to keep power from the hands of the powerless. This is going to be a major Urban League priority in the coming years, and I would like to see the AFL-CIO support our efforts and redouble its own.

Finally, I believe the labor movement can break the zoning restrictions that are primarily responsible for the creation of the white suburban noose around the necks of increasingly black cities. The suburbs are where the new factories and offices are being built. The jobs are going to be at the end of the highway and not in the center of town. But because of zoning restrictions and a refusal to build homes that low and moderate income people can afford, white and black workers will be kept from those jobs. It is in your interest for your members to have access to suburban jobs; and it is in the interests of black people and all Americans to have access to the homes and jobs of suburbia.

BARBARA JORDAN

"WE CAN FORM A NATIONAL COMMUNITY"

Barbara Jordan (1936–   ) has succeeded in accomplishing a number of firsts in government. She was the first African-American woman from a Southern state—in this case, Texas—to serve in the United States Congress and the first black to hold a seat there since 1883.

Not content to rest with these accomplishments, Jordan sponsored Texas's first minimum wage law to include farm workers and others not covered by federal wage standards. She also supported legislation to ban discrimination and to deal with environmental problems.

As a member of the House Judiciary Committee, the Texas Democrat gained national fame in 1974 playing a prominent role during the committee hearings to consider impeachment of President Richard M. Nixon. In 1979, after she had left the House, she joined the faculty of the University of Texas, where she is a professor at the Lyndon B. Johnson School of Public Affairs.

Barbara Jordan's short but illustrious career in government was rewarded in 1976 when she was chosen to be the keynote speaker at the Democratic National Convention. That historic speech, delivered at Madison Square Garden in New York City, is printed below. In it, Jordan explains the principles of America to which her party is committed.

ONE HUNDRED AND FORTY-FOUR YEARS AGO, members of the Democratic Party met for the first time in convention to select their Presidential candidate. Since that time, Democrats have continued to convene once every four years to draft a party platform and nominate a Presidential candidate. Our meeting this week continues that tradition.

There is something different and special about this opening night. I am a keynote speaker.

In the intervening years since 1832, it would have been most unusual for any national political party, to have asked a Barbara Jordan to make a keynote address . . . most unusual.

The past notwithstanding, a Barbara Jordan is before you tonight. This is one additional bit of evidence that the American Dream need not forever be deferred.

Now that I have this distinction, what should I say?

I could easily spend this time praising the accomplishments of this party and attacking the record of the Republicans.

I do not choose to do that.

I could list the many problems which cause people to feel cynical, frustrated, and angry: problems which include the lack of integrity in government; the feeling that the individual no longer counts; the realities of material and spiritual poverty; the feeling that the grand American experiment is failing . . . or has failed. Having described these and other problems, I could sit down without offering any solutions.

I do not choose to do that either.

The citizens of America expect more. They deserve and want more than a recital of problems.

We are a people in a quandry about the present and in search of our future.

We are a people in search of a national community.

It is a search that is unending for we are not only trying to solve the problems of the moment—inflation, unemployment—but on a larger scale, we are attempting to fulfill the promise of America. We are attempting to fulfill our national purpose; to create and sustain a society in which all of us are equal.

Throughout our history, when the people have looked for new ways to uphold the principles upon which this nation rests, they have turned to the political parties. Often they have turned to the Democratic Party.

What is it about the Democratic Party that has made it the instrument through which the people have acted to shape their future?

The answer is our concept of governing which is derived from our view of people. It is a concept rooted in a set of beliefs that are firmly etched in our national consciousness.

What are these beliefs?

First, we believe in equality for all (and) privileges for none. It is a belief that each American, regardless of background, has equal standing in the public forum. Because we believe in this idea, we are an inclusive rather than an exclusive party.

I think it no accident that most of those emigrating to America during the 19th century identified with the Democratic Party. We are a heterogeneous party, made up of Americans with diverse backgrounds.

We believe that the people are the source of governmental power; that the authority of the people is to be extended rather than restricted. This can be accomplished only by providing each citizen with every opportunity to participate in the management of the government.

We believe that the government which represents the authority of *all* the people, not just one interest group, but all the people, has an obligation to *actively* seek to remove those obstacles that block individual achievement . . . obstacles emanating from race, sex, and economic condition.

We are the party of innovation. We do not reject our traditions, but are willing to adapt to changing circumstances. We are willing to suffer the discomfort of change in order to achieve a better future.

We have a positive vision of the future founded on our belief that the gap between the reality and the promise of America can be closed.

This is the bedrock of our concept of governing—the reasons why Americans have turned to the Democratic Party. These are the foundations upon which a national community can be built.

Let all understand that these guiding principles cannot be discharged for short term political gain for they are indigenous to the American idea. They represent what this country is all about. They are not negotiable.

In other times, this exposition of our beliefs would have been sufficient reason for the majority to vote for the nominees of the Democratic Party. Such is not the case today. We have made mistakes. We admit them. In our haste to do all things for all people, we did not foresee the full consequences of our actions. And when the people raised their voices in protest, we did not listen. Our deafness was only a temporary condition and not an irreversible one.

Yet, even as I admit that we have made mistakes, I still believe that as the American people sit in judgment on each party, they will realize that ours were mistakes of the heart.

Now, we must look to the future. Let us heed the voice of the people and recognize their common sense. If we do not, we not only blaspheme our political heritage, we also ignore the common ties that bind Americans.

Many fear the future's uncertainty, are distrustful of their leaders, and believe that their voices are not heard. Many seek only to satisfy their private dreams. They ignore the common interest—the common good.

This is the great danger that American faces, that we will cease to be one nation and become instead a collection of interest groups, each seeking to fulfill private dreams. Each seeking to satisfy private wants.

If this occurs, who then will speak for America?

Who will speak for the common good?

This is the question to be answered in 1976.

Are we to be one people bound together by a common spirit, sharing in a common endeavor or will we become a divided nation: region vs. region; city vs. suburb; interest group against interest group and neighbor against neighbor?

For all of its uncertainty, we cannot flee from the future. We cannot become the new puritans and *reject* our society. We must address and master the future together.

It can be done if we restore the belief that we share a common national endeavor, if we restore our sense of national community.

No Executive Order can require us to form this national community. No federal law can require us to uphold the common good. This we must do as individuals. It will thus be veto-proof.

As a first step, we must restore our belief in ourselves. We are a generous people. Let us be generous with each other and *take to heart* the words spoken by Thomas Jefferson: "Let us restore to social intercourse that harmony and affection without which liberty and even life are but dreary things."

A nation is formed by the willingness of each of us to share in the responsibility for upholding the common good.

A government is invigorated when each of us is willing to participate in the shaping of its future.

In this election year when we must define the common good and begin again to shape our common future, let each person do his or her part. If one citizen is unwilling to participate, we all suffer. For the American idea, though shared by all, is realized in each one of us.

Those of us who are public servants must set the example. It is hypocritical for us to exhort the people to fulfill their duty to the Republic, if we are derelict in ours. More is required of us than slogans, handshakes, and press releases. We must hold ourselves strictly accountable.

If we promise, we must deliver. If we propose, we must produce. If we ask for sacrifice, we must be the first to give. If we make mistakes, we must be willing to admit them.

We must provide the people with a vision of the future that is attainable. We must strike a balance between the idea that the government can do everything and the belief that the government should do nothing.

Let there be no illusions about the difficulty of forming this national community. A spirit of harmony can only survive if each of us remembers when bitterness and self-interest seem to prevail, that we share a common destiny.

I have confidence that we can form a national community.

I have confidence that the Democratic Party *can* lead the way. We cannot improve on the system of government handed down to us by the founders of the Republic, but we can find new ways to implement that system and to realize our destiny.

At the beginning of my remarks, I commented about the uniqueness of a Barbara Jordan speaking to you on this night. I shall conclude by quoting a Republican President and asking you to relate the words of Abraham Lincoln to the concept of a national community in which every last one of us participates:

> As I would not be a slave, so I would not be a master. This expresses my idea of Democracy. Whatever differs from this, to the extent of the difference is no Democracy.

ANGELA Y. DAVIS

"LIFTING AS WE CLIMB"

Angela Y. Davis (1944–   ) was a political activist in the 1970s. Her membership in the Communist party, dismissal from the faculty at the University of California at Los Angeles, and presence at a shootout during a court trial of a friend, Jonathan Jackson, placed her on the FBI's "ten most wanted list." She was finally tried and acquitted of all charges.

Today a celebrated personality, Davis is frequently called upon to speak at special events throughout the country. In her address to the National Women's Studies Association conference at Spelman College in Atlanta, Georgia, June 25, 1987, she explained how "Afro-American women bring to the women's movement a strong tradition of struggle around issues that politically link women to the most crucial progressive causes."

TODAY, AS WE REFLECT on the process of empowering Afro-American women, our most efficacious strategies remain those that are guided by the principle used by Black women in the club movement. We must strive to "lift as we climb." In other words, we must climb in such a way as to guarantee that all of our sisters, regardless of social class, and indeed all of our brothers, climb with us. This must be the essential dynamic of our quest for power—a principle that must not only determine our struggles as Afro-American women, but also govern all authentic struggles of dispossessed people. Indeed, the overall battle for equality can be profoundly enhanced by embracing this principle.

Afro-American women bring to the women's movement a strong tradition of struggle around issues that politically link women to the most crucial progressive causes. This is the meaning of the motto, "Lifting As We Climb." This approach reflects the often unarticulated interests and aspirations of masses of women of all racial backgrounds. Millions of women today are concerned about jobs, working conditions, higher wages, and racist violence. They are concerned about plant closures, homelessness, and repressive immigration legislation. Women are concerned about homophobia, ageism, and discrimination against the physically challenged. We are concerned about Nicaragua and South Africa. And we share our children's dream that tomorrow's world will be delivered from the threat of nuclear omnicide [sic]. These are some of the issues that should be integrated into the overall struggle for women's rights if there is to be a serious commitment to the empowerment of women who have been rendered historically invisible. These are some of the issues we should consider if we wish to lift as we climb.

During this decade we have witnessed an exciting resurgence of the women's movement. If the first wave of the women's movement began in the 1840's, and the second wave in the 1960's, then we are approaching the crest of a third wave in the final days of the 1980's. When the feminist historians of the twenty-first century attempt to recapitulate the third wave, will they ignore the momentous contributions of Afro-American women, who have been leaders and activists in movements often confined to women of color, but whose accomplishments have invariably advanced the cause of white women as well? Will the exclusionary policies of the mainstream women's movement—from its inception to the present—which have often compelled Afro-American women to conduct their struggle for equality outside the ranks of that movement, continue to result in the systematic omission of our names from the roster of prominent leaders and activists of the women's movement? Will there continue to be two distinct continuums of the women's movement, one visible and another invisible, one publicly acknowledged and another ignored except by the conscious progeny of the working-class women—Black, Latina, Native American, Asian, and white—who forged that hidden continuum? If this question is answered in the affirmative, it will mean that women's quest for equality will continue to be gravely deficient. The revolutionary potential of the women's movement still will not have been realized. The racist-inspired flaws of the first and second waves of the women's movement will have become the inherited flaws of the third wave.

How can we guarantee that this historical pattern is broken? As advocates and activists of women's rights in our time, we must begin to merge that double legacy in order to create a single continuum, one that solidly represents the aspirations of all women in our society. We must begin to create a revolutionary, multiracial women's movement that seriously addresses the main issues affecting poor and working-class women. In order to tap the potential for such a movement, we must further develop those sectors of the movement that are addressing seriously issues affecting poor and working-class women, such as jobs, pay equity, paid maternity leave, federally subsidized child care, protection from sterilization abuse, and subsidized abortions. Women of all racial and class backgrounds will greatly benefit from such an approach.

Black women scholars and professionals cannot afford to ignore the straits of our sisters who are acquainted with the immediacy of oppression in a way many of us are not. The process of empowerment cannot be simplistically defined in accordance with our own particular class interests. We must learn to lift as we climb.

When we as Afro-American women, when we as women of color, proceed to ascend toward empowerment, we lift up with us our brothers of color, our white sisters and brothers in the working class, and, indeed, all women who experience the effects of sexist oppression. Our activist agenda must encompass a wide range of demands. We must call for jobs and for the unionization of unorganized women workers, and, indeed, unions must be compelled to take on such issues as affirmative action, pay equity, sexual harassment on the job, and paid maternity leave for women. Because Black and Latina women are AIDS victims in disproportionately large numbers, we have a special interest in demanding emergency funding for AIDS research. We must oppose all instances of repressive mandatory AIDS testing and quarantining, as well as homophobic manipulations of the AIDS crisis. Effective strategies for the reduction of teenage pregnancy are needed, but we must beware of succumbing to propagandistic attempts to relegate to young single mothers the responsibility for our community's impoverishment.

In the aftermath of the Reagan era, it should be clear that there are forces in our society that reap enormous benefits from the persistent, deepening oppression of women. Members of the Reagan administration include advocates for the most racist, antiworking class, and sexist circles of contemporary monopoly capitalism. These corporations continue to prop up apartheid in South Africa and to profit from the spiraling arms race while they propose the most vulgar and irrational forms of anti-

Sovietism—invoking, for example, the "evil empire" image popularized by Ronald Reagan—as justifications for their omnicidal [sic] ventures. If we are not afraid to adopt a revolutionary stance—if, indeed, we wish to be radical in our quest for change—then we must get to the root of our oppression. After all, *radical* simply means "grasping things at the root." Our agenda for women's empowerment must thus be unequivocal in our challenge to monopoly capitalism as a major obstacle to the achievement of equality.

I want to suggest, as I conclude, that we link our grassroots organizing, our essential involvement in electoral politics, and our involvement as activists in mass struggles to the long-range goal of fundamentally transforming the socioeconomic conditions that generate and persistently nourish the various forms of oppression we suffer. Let us learn from the strategies of our sisters in South Africa and Nicaragua. As Afro-American women, as women of color in general, as progressive women of all racial backgrounds, let us join our sisters—and brothers—across the globe who are attempting to forge a new socialist order—an order which will reestablish socioeconomic priorities so that the quest for monetary profit will never be permitted to take precedence over the real interests of human beings. This is not to say that our problems will magically dissipate with the advent of socialism. Rather, such a social order should provide us with the real opportunity to further extend our struggles, with the assurance that one day we will be able to redefine the basic elements of our oppression as useless refuse of the past.

JESSE L. JACKSON

"WE MUST DREAM NEW DREAMS"

A Baptist minister, civil rights activist, and political leader, Jesse L. Jackson (1941–) has emerged as a symbol of America's conscience and a world-famous figure. Jackson trained for the ministry at the Chicago Theological Seminary, then worked with Martin Luther King, Jr., and the Southern Christian Leadership Conference (SCLC), participating in civil rights demonstrations. Eventually he became director of Operation Breadbasket, the economic arm of SCLC, and persuaded many white-owned companies to hire African Americans and to sell products made by African-American manufacturers. It was an idea that Jackson was to develop further in establishing People United to Serve Humanity (PUSH), an organization devoted to gaining economic power for African Americans.

As a presidential candidate for the Democratic party in 1988, Jackson established himself as an eloquent speaker on behalf of women and minorities, and as a critic of the nation's policies and politics. Although failing to win the Democratic nomination in 1984 and 1988, Jackson was a serious contender in both campaigns.

On August 28, 1983, the twentieth anniversary of the historic 1963 March on Washington, Jackson returned to the Lincoln Memorial site to honor Martin Luther King Jr., and recall his dream for African Americans. While much of the dream has yet to be realized, Jackson recognized the many achievements of African Americans and identified the many achievements needed for King's dream to become a reality.

TWENTY YEARS AGO, Dr. Martin Luther King, Jr., had a dream of freedom for all Americans. Twenty years later the power of his dream has drawn this generation together and inspires us to keep on dreaming. We must continue to dream, but the dream of 1963 must be expanded to meet the realities of these times. We must dream new dreams, expand the horizons of our dreams to meet the realities of these times, and remove any ceiling or barrier that would limit our legitimate aspirations. Democracy at its best provides a floor for everyone—but imposes limits upon no one. The sky is the limit. Let us continue to dream. Dreaming is a gift of the spirit that can lift you above misery to miracles and allow you to smile through tears.

Twenty years ago, we came to these hallowed grounds as a rainbow coalition to demand our freedom. Twenty years later, we have our freedom—our civil rights. On our way to Washington today we didn't have to stop at a friend's house or a church to eat or use the bathroom. Apartheid is over. But, twenty years later, we still do not have equality. We have moved in. Now we must move up.

Twenty years ago, we were stripped of our dignity. Twenty years later, we are stripped of our share of power. The absence of segregation is not the presence of social justice or equality.

Twenty years ago, there were no blacks in Congress or in statewide offices in the nine southern states where 53 percent of blacks live.

Twenty years later, we still have none, because the Voting Rights Act has been sabotaged. It has been reduced to an Indian treaty—an unfulfilled law. The Democratic party is violating the law. The Republican party is not enforcing the law. We're still looking for allies who will be fair as our struggle shifts from welfare to our share—from aid to trade, from social generosity to economic reciprocity.

Twenty years ago, there were fewer than 400 black elected officials in the land. Twenty years later, we have 5,200—but that constitutes only 1 percent of the 512,000 officials in this nation. We are still more than 50,000 short of our share. And at the present rate—1 percent every 18 years—it will take us 198 years to achieve equality.

Twenty years later, no longer do the blatant forms of voting rights denial dominate the news—poll taxes, grandfather clauses, literacy tests, and violence. Now the new forms of voter denial go unreported—dual registration, second primaries, gerrymandering, annexation, at-large elections, and registrars who function arbitrarily. The forms of voter denial are different, but the effect is the same.

In Mississippi, blacks are 40 percent of the population. Yet, of five members of Congress, none is black; of nine Supreme Court Justices, none is black; of eight statewide officials, none is black; of eighty-two tax assessors, one is black; of eighty-two registrars, two are black; of eighty-two sheriffs, three are black. The pattern is the same in Virginia, North Carolina, South Carolina, Georgia, Florida, Alabama, Louisiana, and Arkansas. We want our share.

We must defend the poor—the boats stuck on the

bottom. Mississippi is still the litmus test of democracy, the Democrats, and the Justice Department. We cannot measure our progress by a few more captains on ships on high seas. We must focus on the masses of boats stuck on the bottom. If the boats stuck on the bottom can rise, all of us will rise.

If the boats stuck on the bottom rise, corporate America will be held accountable; the Equal Rights Amendment will rise; health, education, and housing programs will rise; peace, jobs, and a clean and safe environment will rise; those at the sunrise of life, our young, and those in the sunset of life, our elderly, will rise.

If the boats stuck on the bottom can rise, blacks and Hispanics and women can go to Congress, progressive candidates—whites, blacks, Hispanics, and women—can go to the Senate, and collectively we can determine who will go to the White House.

Twenty years ago, we were together, and we made progress. Twenty years later, apart, there has been regression. On this day, we must revive our coalition. We must remind each other from where we have come, forgive each other, redeem each other, and look to the future. We have proven that we can survive without one another, but we have not proven that we can win without each other. The rainbow coalition must be resurrected.

* * *

But the rainbow coalition of the rejected cannot accept the status quo. We must have a new vision. At home, we must fight for one set of rules—equal protection under the law. Abroad, we must measure human rights by one yardstick. We can't define democracy as majority rule in North America and as minority rule in South Africa.

We can't impose economic sanctions in Poland because of martial law and then become South Africa's number-one trading partner. We just want the game played by one set of rules. We must choose the human race over the nuclear race. El Salvador is our neighbor, not our nemesis. They are our next-door neighbor, not our back-door threat.

The rainbow coalition must seek new values and a new world order. Twenty years ago, blacks, Hispanics, youth, and the military were denied the right to vote. But, twenty years later, American democracy has made a marvelous adjustment—it has made room for all of us. Now we don't have to explode through riots or implode through drugs. We can seek change through orderly elections and not through bloody revolutions. The rainbow coalition represents promise and power, but we must focus on the strength and courage of David, not just on the tyranny of Goliath. The repressive Reagan regime won because David did not use all of his political rocks and his slingshot. David has unused rocks just lying around. Goliath won with a perverse coalition of the rich and the unregistered.

What do I mean? In the North, Reagan won Massachusetts by 2,500 votes, but there were 64,000 unregistered blacks; he won Illinois by 176,000, with 600,000 unregistered blacks; he won Delaware by 5,400, with 20,000 unregistered blacks; and he won New York by 165,000, with 900,000 unregistered blacks.

In the South, Reagan won Alabama by 17,000, with 272,000 unregistered blacks; he won Arkansas by 5,000, with 85,000 unregistered blacks; Kentucky by 17,000, with 62,000 unregistered blacks; Louisiana by 84,000, with 256,000 unregistered blacks; Mississippi by 11,000, with 131,000 unregistered blacks; North Carolina by 39,000, with 505,000 unregistered blacks; South Carolina by 11,000, with 292,000 unregistered blacks; Tennessee by 4,700, with 158,000 unregistered blacks.

He won these eight southern states—states with 72 electoral votes, 27 percent of what he needed to win— with a cumulative total of 192,000 votes—and there are

3,000,000 unregistered black voters in the South alone! Rocks just lying around.

But we've changed our mind. He won Mississippi by 11,000 votes in 1980, but we've registered 40,000 new Mississippi voters since May. Hands that picked cotton in 1964 will pick a president in 1984.

* * *

If we will but hold on, God has promised us a rainbow after the flood—the Reagan flood of a denial of jobs, peace, and freedom. There is a balm in Gilead. He has given us a formula—turn to each other, not on each other. Separately, we may be poor, but when we come together we aren't poor any more. We have been born and bred in the slums, but the slums are not born and bred in us.

David, don't let Goliath break your spirit! Hold on to your dreams! Don't give up! Hold on to your dreams! Use what you've got. Don't complain about what you don't have. Hold on to your dreams! David, pick up your rocks. Stand up! Stand tall! Stand proud! Use your rocks. Little David, your time has come.

Make up your mind. There is nothing more powerful than a made-up mind. Run toward freedom! Don't stand still! Run! Steal away to freedom! Run! You may lose if you run, but you're guaranteed to lose if you don't. Run! At the worst you'll gain your self-respect, and at the best you'll help to save a nation. Run! Take the chains off of your ankles, but don't shift them to your mind. Run! Run from disgrace to amazing grace. Run! Run from the outhouse to the statehouse to the courthouse to the White House. Run! But hold on to your dreams.

END NOTES

1. W.E.B Du Bois, *The Souls of Black Folk* (New York: Fawcett, 1961), p. 17.
2. Ibid., p. 141.
3. David Walker, *Walker's Appeal*, in *Four Articles, Together with Preamble, to the Colored Citizens of the World, but in Particular, and Very Expressly to Those of the United States of America,"* in Herbert Aptheker, ed., *One Continual Cry* (New York: Humanities Press, 1965), pp. 63–68.
4. Carl Schurz, *A Report on Reconstruction*, 39th Congress, 1st Session, Senate Executive Document 2 (1865) pp. 16–20.
5. "Black Power," in Joanne Grant, ed., *Black Protest: History, Documents, and Analyses, 1619 to the Present* (New York: Fawcett, 1968), pp. 459–466.
6. Booker T. Washington, "Atlanta Exposition Address," in Booker T. Washington, *Up from Slavery* (New York: Penguin Books, 1986), pp. 218–225.

7. A. Philip Randolph, speech delivered to the Society for Ethical Culture, New York, September 2, 1956.

8. Frederick Douglass, "Three Addresses on the Relations Subsisting Between the White and Colored People of the United States," in Philip S. Foner, ed., *The Voice of Black America* (New York: Simon and Schuster, 1972), pp. 491–494.

9. Jermain Wesley Loguen, *J. W. Loguen, As a Slave and As a Freeman: A Narrative of Real Life*, in Philip S. Foner, ed, *The Voice of Black America* (New York: Simon and Schuster, 1972), pp. 98–99.

10. Marcus Garvey, "The Principles of the Universal Negro Improvement Association," in Amy Jacques-Garvey, ed., *Philosophy and Opinions of Marcus Garvey, or Africa for the Africans* (New York: Atheneum, 1911), p. 95–97.

11. Ibid.

THE SOURCES OF
THE SPEECHES

I

David Walker, Jr., *David Walker's Appeal, in Four Articles, Together with Preamble to the Colored Citizens of the World, But in Particular, and Very Expressly to Those of the United States of America*, in Herbert Aptheker, ed., *One Continual Cry* (New York: Humanities Press, 1965), pp. 63–68.

Peter Williams, Jr., "Slavery and Colonization," in Carter G. Woodson, ed., *Negro Orators and Their Orations* (Washington, D.C., 1925), pp. 77–81.

James Forten, Sr., "The Negro Abolitionist," in Leslie H. Fishel and Benjamin Quarles, eds., *The Black American—A Documentary History* (New York: William Morrow, 1970), pp. 191–193.

Jermain Wesley Loguen, *The Rev. J. W. Loguen, As a Slave and As a Freeman: A Narrative of Real Life*, in Philip S. Foner, ed., *The Voice of Black America* (New York: Simon and Schuster, 1972), pp. 98–100. Original text in *As a Slave and As a Freeman: A Nar-*

rative of Real Life (Syracuse: J. G. E Truair & Co., 1859).

John Sweat Rock, "Negro Hopes for Emancipation," in Philip S. Foner, ed., *The Voice of Black America* (New York: Simon and Schuster, 1972), pp. 251–256. Original text in *Liberator*, February 14, 1862.

II

Sojourner Truth, "When Women Gets Her Rights Man Will Be Right," in Philip S. Foner, ed., *The Voice of Black America* (New York: Simon and Schuster, 1972), pp. 345–347. Original text in *National Anti-Slavery Standard*, June 1, 1867.

Robert B. Elliott, "Civil Rights—Speech of Hon. Robert B. Elliott of South Carolina in the House of Representatives," in Philip S. Foner, ed., *The Voice of Black America* (New York: Simon and Schuster, 1972), pp. 385–386. Original text in [untitled pamphlet] (Washington, D.C.: Beardsley & Snodgrass, January 6, 1874).

Blanche Kelso Bruce, "Negro Hopes for Assimilation," in Mortimer J. Adler, Charles Van Doren, George Ducas, eds., *The Negro in American History* II (New York: Encyclopedia Britannica Educational Corporation, 1972), pp. 225–229. Original text in *Congressional Record*, 44 Congress, 1 Session, 3/31/1876, pp. 2101–2105.

Frederick Douglass, "Three Addresses on the Relations Subsisting Between the White and Colored People of the United States," in Philip S. Foner, ed., *The Voice of Black America* (New York: Simon and Schuster, 1972), pp. 491–494. Original text in [untitled] (Washington, D.C.: Gibson Bros. Printers and Binders, 1886).

Mary Church Terrell, "The Progress of Colored Women," in Philip S. Foner, ed., *The Voice of Black America* (New York: Simon and Schuster, 1972), pp. 643–647.

Original text in *The Voice of the Negro*, July 1904, pp. 292–294.

III

Booker T. Washington, "Atlanta Exposition Address," in Booker T. Washington, *Up from Slavery* (New York: Penguin Books, 1986), pp. 218–225.

Ida B. Wells-Barnett, "Text from the Proceedings of the National Negro Conference," 1909, pp. 174–179.

Marcus Garvey, "The Principles of the Universal Negro Improvement Association," in Amy Jacques-Garvey, ed., *Philosophy and Opinions of Marcus Garvey, or Africa for the Africans* (New York: Atheneum, 1977), pp. 95–97.

W.E.B. Du Bois, "Disfranchisement," New York: National Women's Suffrage Association, 1912.

IV

James Baldwin, "A Talk to Teachers," in James Baldwin, *The Price of the Ticket* (New York: St. Martin's Press, 1985), pp. 325–332.

Martin Luther King, Jr., "I Have a Dream," in Ed. Clayton, ed., *Martin Luther King: The Peaceful Warrior* (New York: Pocket Books, 1968), pp. 110–118. Original text in *The SCLC Story in Words and Pictures*, 1964, pp. 50–51.

Malcolm X, "Address to Mississippi Youth," in *Malcolm X Speaks—Selected Speeches and Statements* (New York: Pathfinder, 1965), pp. 137–145.

Stokely Carmichael, "Stokely Carmichael on Black Power," in Marvin E. Gettleman, ed., *Black Protest—History, Documents, and Analyses, 1619 to the Present* (New York: Fawcett Premier, 1968), pp. 459–466. Original speech in transcribed taped remarks, University of California at Berkeley, November 19, 1966.

Shirley Chisholm (no title given), in *Congressional Record*, 91st Congress, 1st Session, pp. H2242–2243.

James Forman, "Black Manifesto," in Action Training Clearing House Notes, Metropolitan Urban Service Training (MUST), New York City, May 4, 1969, pp. 1157–1161.

V

Vernon F. Jordan, Jr.,"Black People and the Unions," in *Vital Speeches of the Day*, January 1, 1972.

Barbara Jordan, *Keynote Speech 1976 Democratic National Convention*, Press Release, July 12, 1976, New York City.

Angela Y. Davis, "Radical Perspectives on Empowerment for Afro-American Women," in Angela Davis, *Women, Culture, and Politics* (New York: Random House, 1989), pp. 5–14. Original text in *Harvard Educational Review*, March 8, 1988.

Jesse L. Jackson, "Dreaming New Dreams," in Roger Hatch and Frank E. Watkins, eds., *Reverend Jesse L. Jackson—Straight from the Heart* (Philadelphia: Augsburg Fortress, 1987), pp. 19–22.

FOR FURTHER READING

Bruce, Blanche Kelso (1841–1898)
Sterling, Philip. *Four Took Freedom*. Garden City, N.Y.: Doubleday, 1967.

Carmichael, Stokely (1941–   )
Carmichael, Stokely, and Charles V. Hamilton. *Black Power*. New York: Vintage Books, 1967.

Chisholm, Shirley (1924–   )
The Good Fight. New York: Harper and Row, 1973.
Unbought and Unbossed. Boston: Houghton Mifflin, 1970.
Haskins, James. *Fighting Shirley Chisholm*. New York: Dial, 1975.

Davis, Angela Y. (1941–   )
Angela Davis: An Autobiography. New York: International Publishers, 1988.

Women, Race and Class. New York: Vintage Books, 1983.

Olden, Marc. *Angla Davis.* New York: Lancer Books, 1973.

Douglass, Frederick (1817–1895)

Narrative of the Life of Frederick Douglass. Cambridge, Mass.: The Belknap Press of Harvard University Press, 1960.

An American Slave Written by Himself. Benjamin Quarles, ed. Cambridge, Mass.: Harvard University Press, 1960.

Bontemp, Arna. *Free At Last—The Life of Frederick Douglass.* New York: Dodd, Mead, 1971.

Huggins, Nathan Irvin. *Slave and Citizen—The Life of Frederick Douglass.* Boston: Little, Brown, 1980.

McKissack, Patricia. *Frederick Douglass, The Black Lion.* Chicago: Children's Press, 1989.

Miller, Douglass T. *Frederick Douglass and the Flight for Freedom.* New York: Facts on File, 1988.

Preston, Dickson J. *Young Frederick Douglass—The Maryland Years.* Baltimore: Johns Hopkins, 1988.

Du Bois, W.E.B. 1868–1963.

The Souls of Black Folk. Greenwich, Conn.: Fawcett, 1961.

Logan, Rayford, ed. *W.E.B. Du Bois—A Profile.* New York: Hill and Wang, 1971.

Hamilton, Virginia. *W.E.B. DuBois: A Biography.* New York: Crowell, 1972.

McKissack, Patricia, and Frederick McKissack. *W.E.B. Du Bois.* New York: Franklin Watts, 1989.

Stafford, Mark. *W.E.B. Du Bois.* New York: Chelsea House, 1989.

Sterne, Emma Gelders. *His Was the Voice—The Life*

of W.E.B. Du Bois. New York: Crowell-Collier, 1971.

Forman, James (1929–)
   The Making of Black Revolutionaries—A Personal Account. Washington D.C.: Open Hand, 1985.

Forten, James, Sr. (1766–1842)
   Douty, Esther (Morris). *Forten, the Sailmaker*. Chicago: Rand McNally, 1968.

Garvey, Marcus (1887–1940)
   Jacques-Garvey, Amy, ed. *Philosophy and Opinions of Marcus Garvey*. New York: Atheneum, 1969.
   Cronon, Edmund David. *Marcus Garvey—The Story of Marcus Garvey*. Madison, Wis.: 1969.
   Davis, Daniel S. *Marcus Garvey*. New York: Franklin Watts, 1972.
   Jacques-Garvey, Mary. *Garvey and Garveyism*. New York: Collier Books, 1970.
   Martin, Tony. *Marcus Garvey, Hero*. Dover, Md.: The Majority Press, 1983.

Jackson, Jesse L. (1941–)
   Strength to Love. Philadelphia: Fortress Press, 1963.
   Chaplik, Dorothy. *Up with Hope: A Biography of Jesse Jackson*. Minneapolis: Dillon, 1986.
   Colton, Elizabeth O. *The Jackson Phenomenon—The Man, the Power and the Message*. New York: Doubleday, 1989.
   Kosof, Anna. *Jesse Jackson*. New York: Franklin Watts, 1987.
   McKissack, Patricia C. *Jesse Jackson: A Biography*. New York: Scholastic, 1989.
   Stone, Eddie. *Jesse Jackson*. Los Angeles: Holloway House, 1979.

Jordan, Barbara (1936–   )
Barbara Jordan. New York: Doubleday, 1979.
Haskins, James. *Barbara Jordan.* New York: Scholastic, 1977.

King, Martin Luther, Jr. (1929–1968)
Bennett, Lerone. *What Manner of Man.* Chicago: Johnson Publishers, 1964; New York: Simon and Schuster, 1968.
Clayton, Ed. *The Peaceful Warrior.* New York: Pocket Books, 1968.
Haskins, James. *The Life and Death of Martin Luther King, Jr.* New York: Lothrop, 1977.
Schulke, Flip, and Penelope McPhee. *King Remembered.* New York: Pocket Books, 1986.

Loguen, Jermain Wesley (1813–1872)
The Rev. J. W. Loguen, as a Slave and as a Freeman: A Narrative of Real Life. New York: Negro Universities Press, 1968.

Malcolm X (1925–1905)
Malcolm X Speaks—Selected Speeches and Statements. New York: Pathfinder, 1965.
The Autobiography of Malcolm X. With Alex Haley. New York: Grove Press, 1975.
Lomax, Louis E. *To Kill a Black Man.* Los Angeles, 1968.
White, Florence M. *Malcolm X: Black and Proud.* Champaign, Ill.: Garrard, 1975.

Terrell, Mary Church (1863–1954)
Sterling, Dorothy. *Mary Church Terrell—Lift Every Voice.* New York: Doubleday, 1965.

Truth, Sojourner (1797–1883)
Bernard, Jacqueline. *Journey Toward Freedom.* New York, 1967.

Claflin, Edward Beecher. *Sojourner Truth and the Struggle for Freedom*. New York: Barron's, 1987.

Ferris, Jeri. *Walking the Road to Freedom—A Story about Sojourner Truth*. Minneapolis: Carolrhoda, 1988.

Krass, Peter. *Sojourner Truth*. New York: Chelsea House, 1988.

Ortiz, Victoria. *A Self-Made Woman*. New York and Philadelphia: Lippincott, 1974.

Walker, David (1785–1830)

David Walker's Appeal, in Four Articles, Together with a Preamble, to the Colored Citizens of the World, But in Particular, and Very Expressly to Those of the United States of America. New York: Hill and Wang, 1965.

Walker, A., and James Haskins. *Double Dutch*. Hillside, N.J.: Enslow Publishers, 1986.

Washington, Booker T. (1856–1915)

Up from Slavery. New York: Viking, 1956, and Airmont Books, 1967.

Harlan, Louis R. *The Making of a Black Leader 1856–1901*. New York: Oxford University Press, 1972.

Kaye, Tony. *Booker T. Washington*. New York: Chelsea House, 1989.

Wells-Barnett, Ida B. (1862–1931)

Crusade for Justice. Chicago: University of Chicago Press, 1970.

Sterling, Dorothy. *Black Foremothers*. Old Westbury, N.Y.: Feminist Press, 1979.

INDEX

189